KEEP GOING

ALSO BY THE AUTHOR

Keep Teaching
Everyday Genesis
Hunting Hope
Twelve Clean Pages

KEEP GOING

NIKA MAPLES

bel esprit books
Dallas | Fort Worth

KEEP GOING

Copyright © 2019 by Nika Maples

Published by Bel Esprit Books, LLC
PO Box 821801
North Richland Hills, TX 76182

All rights reserved. Printed in the United States of America. No part of this book may be reproduced, stored in a retrieval system, or transmitted in any form and by any means—electronic, mechanical, photocopy, recording, or any other—except in the case of brief quotations in reviews, without written permission of the author.

Scripture quotations marked (CJB) are taken from the Complete Jewish Bible by David H. Stern. Copyright © 1998. All rights reserved. Used by permission of Messianic Jewish Publishers, 6120 Day Long Lane, Clarksville, MD 21029. www.messianicjewish.net.

Scripture quotations marked (ESV) are taken from the English Standard Version®. Text Edition: 2016. Copyright © 2001 by Crossway, a publishing ministry of Good News Publishers. The ESV® text has been reproduced in cooperation with and by permission of Good News Publishers. Unauthorized reproduction of this publication is prohibited. All rights reserved.

Scripture quotations marked (NKJV) are taken from the New King James Version®. Copyright © 1982 by Thomas Nelson. Used by permission. All rights reserved.

Scripture quotations marked (NIV) are taken from THE HOLY BIBLE, NEW INTERNATIONAL VERSION®, NIV® Copyright © 1973, 1978, 1984, 2011 by Biblica, Inc.® Used by permission. All rights reserved worldwide.

Scripture quotations marked (NLT) are taken from the Holy Bible, New Living Translation. Copyright © 1996, 2004, 2007 by Tyndale House Foundation. Used by permission of Tyndale House Publishers, Inc., Carol Stream, Illinois 60188. All rights reserved.

Scripture quotations marked (MSG) are taken from The Message. Copyright © 1993, 1994, 1995, 1996, 2000, 2001, 2002. Used by permission of NavPress Publishing Group.

Cover and interior design and typesetting: Kent Jensen | knail.com

Back cover photo: Wren Maples | Sugar Maple Portraits

Copy editing (and brilliant, heartfelt insight): Christi Romeo

ISBN: 978-1-7331734-2-1

First Edition: December 2019

TO

Everyone whose wait
is taking longer than you thought

CONTENTS

The Bird in the Mirror	ix
JANUARY | KINDNESS	1
FEBRUARY | GOODNESS	33
MARCH | FAITHFULNESS	63
APRIL | GENTLENESS	95
MAY | SELF-CONTROL	127
JUNE | REST	159
JULY | RENEWAL	191
AUGUST | PREPARATION	223
SEPTEMBER | LOVE	255
OCTOBER | JOY	287
NOVEMBER | PEACE	319
DECEMBER | PATIENCE	351
About the Author	383

THE BIRD IN THE MIRROR

The journal was already open on my lap, and I reached for a pen as tears began to fall. Every time the Texas autumn was cool enough, I would sit in a rocking chair on my small front porch and have some intentional moments with the Lord.

For months, I had been waiting on something I thought God was going to bring to pass. When it still hadn't happened, I blamed myself. Surely I had done something wrong, taken a misstep, failed to turn around the right corner. Before I began to write through my anger, self-blame, and confusion, I asked the Holy Spirit what He wanted to say to me.

Just then, I heard a sound that would happen again and again over the coming days, and would profoundly touch and teach my soul.

There was a loud knocking, and I looked up.

A bird, a beautiful male cardinal, was diving into the passenger side mirror of a sedan parked in the driveway across the street. His red wings beat wildly. He pummeled the passenger mirror again and again, sometimes with the thud of his head, sometimes with the crack of his beak.

I had seen birds fly into windows before, thinking the reflection was the sky. But this bird flew into a *mirror*, thinking his reflection was the enemy.

I pondered the strange bird for a moment. Then I went on, writing my anguished prayer, asking the Holy Spirit what He wanted to say to me.

The next morning, I went out on the porch to read the Bible and pray, and there was the bird. He was more aggressive this time. I noticed his taupe-feathered female friend in a tree nearby. I wondered, *Is there a nest? If so, he has left it unprotected in order to fight against himself.*

On the third day, I went out on the porch again, but this time, during the evening hours. I still had so much frustration at myself, and I just needed the Holy Spirit to speak clearly and give me direction.

Again, there was the bird.

His mate called to him from the branches, while he continued to bang his head. I couldn't believe that this crazed cardinal was there once again.

That poor bird! Something's wrong with him! I thought, *He keeps returning to this spot to attack himself.*

And with that, I finally understood.

Yes, he was coming back day after day, but who else was coming back day after day, asking the same questions and not listening to the answers?

I was.

Sometimes, I am that bird, hitting my head against my own reflection, complaining about my life instead of living it.

On the fourth day, the bird was there again. And I thought about asking the neighbor to put something over that mirror so that he wouldn't continue to harm himself.

But then the cardinal did something he hadn't done

on previous days. He moved on to the next driveway and car. And then he moved on to the next. He slammed into mirror after mirror, as his mate chased him. From my place on the rocker, I could hear his knocking echo from all the way down the block.

The Holy Spirit's voice was unmistakable:

There will always be another mirror for the person who wants to find fault in himself.

Seeing that bird brought grief, both for him and for me, because there I was, fighting my self-image the way the bird fought his image. In blaming myself, I wasn't moving forward in what God had for me.

I was paralyzed.

Self-blame and responsibility are two different things. That is because self-blame is rooted in fear, and responsibility is rooted in courage. Blaming and taking responsibility are both active responses that are empowered by emotions. Any response that is fed by fear will lead to personal paralysis. Any response that is nourished by courage will lead us to keep going.

It was the idea of nourishing with courage that prompted this book.

Keep Going is an adaptation of my devotional book for educators, *Keep Teaching*. I wrote the manuscript for *Keep Teaching* just after that long and frustrating wait, when I saw the bird in the mirror. As a response to seeing the cardinal, I had started moving forward by choice, through intentionally reading Scripture out loud over my life. At the same time, I started writing a devotional filled with verses that teachers could read out loud over their empty classrooms.

When *Keep Teaching* finally released, it immediately sold more than I expected, and the positive response was overwhelming. Teachers told me they had never read the Bible out loud over their life and work, and they were seeing small changes every day.

And then something else happened.

People who were *not* educators were contacting me, hoping I would write a devotional that was like *Keep Teaching* but could be used by anyone.

It was an idea I couldn't let go.

I know I am not the only one who has banged my head into a mirror, so to speak. There are plenty of us who confuse self-blame with responsibility. That is because a long wait is hard, and the first thing we do is start looking for ways we must have messed things up.

The next thing we do is give up.

My prayer is that your *Keep Going* devotional book will be one of the ways you choose to walk away from the mirror. By reading the Word of God over yourself daily, may you be reminded not to look at your situation through your own eyes.

But through His.

JANUARY

MEDITATIONS ON KINDNESS

Here is a simple, rule-of-thumb guide for behavior: Ask yourself what you want people to do for you, then grab the initiative and do it for them.

Matthew 7:12a (MSG)

JANUARY 1

READ OUT LOUD: **Matthew 6:33 (NLT)**

Seek the Kingdom of God above all else, and live righteously, and he will give you everything you need.

Any time you want to transition into new habits and frames of mind, what you really want is power—the power to improve and live life better.

The more you seek personal and professional goals, the greater the potential for the Kingdom of God to fall in priority. This year, make sure the Kingdom stays first on your list of pursuits. Keeping the Kingdom first will give you the power you need for everything, be it achieving a great goal or increasing your ability to show consistent, daily kindness.

Seek Kingdom empowerment for all things.
It takes more effort than you think to be kind.

PRAY AND LISTEN TO THE LORD. LIST FIVE THINGS HE MIGHT BE LEADING YOU TO IMPROVE THIS YEAR.

1. _____
2. _____
3. _____
4. _____
5. _____

JANUARY 2

READ OUT LOUD: Ecclesiastes 8:17 (NLT)

I realized that no one can discover everything God is doing under the sun. Not even the wisest people discover everything, no matter what they claim.

Have you ever thought of humility as a kindness? Always take a position of humility. Realize that you don't know it all.

Humility is refreshing, and it tempers the climate in your relationships. One way you can show humility is to ask genuine questions. Be careful how you ask them, though. Questions from a prideful person feel like a white-hot lamp of interrogation. But questions that come from a humble heart feel like a cool breeze.

How can you show friends and family humility?

- Show them you never want to assume what they think or prefer.
- Show them you *still* want to get to know them better, even after all these years.
- Show them that growing in discernment is a forever-journey, and you want them to walk beside you toward greater understanding.

Show them that questions are a *quest* for connection.

JANUARY 3

READ OUT LOUD: **Matthew 5:19b (NIV)**

... whoever practices and teaches these commands will be called great in the kingdom of heaven.

The way you interact teaches those around you what you really believe about kindness. It is one thing to say you value kindness and another thing to actually be kind. Plenty of people are willing to *talk* about kindness, and few are intentional about consistently walking it out. Kindness doesn't seem like something we should take seriously.

But the enemy wants you to stop paying attention to the kindness of your actions, to stop living out what you say.

The enemy has two strategies, plain and simple.
If he can't make you *quit*, he will make you a *hypocrite*.

THANK THE LORD FOR THREE SMALL KINDNESSES THAT YOU HAVE RECEIVED FROM OTHERS IN THE LAST FEW WEEKS.

1. _____
2. _____
3. _____

JANUARY 4

READ OUT LOUD: **Ephesians 4:29 (CJB)**

Let no harmful language come from your mouth, only good words that are helpful in meeting the need, words that will benefit those who hear them.

God gave you phenomenal power when He gave you a mouth that can speak. But He also gave you a choice about *what* to speak. Your words can either tear down or build up. Not every thought in your head is kind. Not every thought in your head needs to be spoken.

Carefully consider which of your thoughts should take root. Words are seeds. When your thoughts become words, they are planted in another person's heart, and they will grow until they blossom.

Make sure the seeds you plant are kind ones.

MAKE A LIST OF FIVE WORD-SEEDS THAT YOU WANT TO PLANT IN YOUR OWN LIFE. BEGIN EACH SENTENCE WITH *I AM*. CHOOSE YOUR WORDS WISELY BECAUSE WHAT YOU PLANT WILL GROW.

1. I AM _____
2. I AM _____
3. I AM _____
4. I AM _____
5. I AM _____

JANUARY 5

READ OUT LOUD: Ephesians 4:29 (NLT)

Don't use foul or abusive language. Let everything you say be good and helpful, so that your words will be an encouragement to those who hear them.

When God saw the earth He had created, He said three simple words: *It is good.*

Just three words.

Some people never have the pleasure of hearing affirming words. A healthy economy of positive words from you can eternally change the friend, colleague, or employee who has been living in a poverty of encouragement, never having enough.

It doesn't take much to satisfy their hunger. It just takes small and steady kindnesses.

Don't decide not to give *anything* just because you are not in the position to give *a lot.*

LIST A FEW "THREE WORD PHRASES" THAT CAN BE LIFE-CHANGING TO THE LISTENER. (EXAMPLES: I AM HERE, YOU ARE MINE, ETC.)

1. _____
2. _____
3. _____
4. _____

JANUARY 6

READ OUT LOUD: **Matthew 19:13-15 (NIV)**

Then people brought little children to Jesus for him to place his hands on them and pray for them. But the disciples rebuked them. Jesus said, "Let the little children come to me, and do not hinder them, for the kingdom of heaven belongs to such as these."

Jesus called to the vulnerable.

He was a refuge for them, a safe place, a covering.

No harsh words could rain on others when Jesus was nearby.

Be the same way. Let your words to those around you be soft and well-meaning, words that ride on a smile.

Even correction can be kind.

IMAGINE YOU HAVE TO CORRECT SOMEONE TODAY. PRACTICE CORRECTING IN THE KINDEST WAY BY WRITING OUT WHAT YOU WOULD SAY.

_____

_____

_____

_____

_____

_____

JANUARY 7

READ OUT LOUD: **Ephesians 4:32 (NKJV)**

And be kind to one another, tenderhearted, forgiving one another, even as God in Christ forgave you.

Unforgiveness is a dark and double-locked door. Not only does it hold *you* back, it also may hold back the other person.

There is nothing kind about being unforgiving. Unforgiveness is what people fear most. They hope you will be able to forgive the worst things they have done.

You are made in the image of God. Therefore, your attitudes and actions can give other people an idea of what He is like.

God forgives.

If the road back to your heart after an offense is a cracked-glass street rather than a petal-soft pathway, then few will be willing to walk it. And if they choose to stay away from *you*—a representative of God here on earth—then it won't be long before they choose to stay away from God Himself.

Misrepresenting God's kind heart causes tragic consequences for the people who are watching you, hoping to catch a glimpse of *Him*.

JANUARY 8

READ OUT LOUD: Galatians 6:4-5 (NLT)

Pay careful attention to your own work, for then you will get the satisfaction of a job well done, and you won't need to compare yourself to anyone else. For we are each responsible for our own conduct.

It is one thing to have information and experience; it is another to apply them. The application of information and experience is called *wisdom*. Wisdom is always kind.

When your information and experience suddenly make you want to speak into someone's life, ask yourself if it is wise to do so.

Most people can give their full attention to only one voice at a time.

The Holy Spirit is a better communicator than you are.

Sometimes it is wise to reserve your comments so that other people can hear His voice over yours.

THANK GOD FOR A TIME WHEN YOU HEARD HIS VOICE OVER ALL OTHER NOISE.

_____

_____

_____

_____

JANUARY 9

READ OUT LOUD: Galatians 6:4-5 (MSG)

Make a careful exploration of who you are and the work you have been given, and then sink yourself into that. Don't be impressed with yourself. Don't compare yourself with others. Each of you must take responsibility for doing the creative best you can with your own life.

Try not to misinterpret your responsibilities, taking on more than what is yours.

Be kind to yourself.
Mind your own business.

ASK GOD TO GIVE YOU THE STRENGTH NOT TO TAKE ON MORE THAN WHAT IS YOURS.

JANUARY 10

READ OUT LOUD: 1 Peter 4:10-11 (NLT)

God has given each of you a gift from his great variety of spiritual gifts. Use them well to serve one another. Do you have the gift of speaking? Then speak as though God Himself were speaking through you. Do you have the gift of helping others? Do it with all the strength and energy that God supplies. Then everything you do will bring glory to God through Jesus Christ. All glory and power to him forever and ever! Amen.

God has so many spiritual gifts to give. He has not left anyone out. The spiritual gifts He has given you are treasures you can give to others.

In the Old Testament, King David called the people of Israel to bring earthly treasures as offerings to build the temple. Out of the kindness of their hearts, the people brought all they had. And together they had more than enough.

Out of the kindness of your heart, you can bring heavenly treasures—your spiritual gifts—as offerings to build up and bless your home and workplace.

If everyone brings all they have, there will be more than enough.

JANUARY 11

READ OUT LOUD: **Proverbs 11:24-25 (NLT)**

Give freely and become more wealthy; be stingy and lose everything. The generous will prosper; those who refresh others will themselves be refreshed.

If you are exhausted, think of some way to refresh another person. This is God's law of reciprocation.

Refreshment for others is linked to refreshment for you.

Reach out to another in kindness, and the reward will be yours.

Try it.
Test it.

WRITE ONE THING YOU CAN DO TO REFRESH SOMEONE THIS WEEK.

_____

_____

THANK GOD FOR SOMETHING THAT SOMEONE HAS DONE TO REFRESH YOU THIS WEEK.

_____

_____

JANUARY 12

READ OUT LOUD: **Proverbs 16:28 (NIV)**

A perverse person stirs up conflict, and a gossip separates close friends.

Ask God to do a simple thing today.

Ask Him to put a seat belt around you.

Then the next time you are tempted to say something you shouldn't, you will feel that gentle pressure. You will feel the seat belt God is using to restrain you and keep you safe.

Do not be sidetracked by the grapevine. Gossip usually leads to a relationship wreck with injuries.

When drivers see a car wreck on the highway, they tend to *rubberneck*, drawing their attention away from what's ahead of them and toward the scene of the accident.

In the same way, everyone will stare at a broken or struggling relationship instead of looking after what God has placed in front of them. That is the last thing you want. Speak kindly at all times. Beware of gossip.

Avoid rubbernecking at relationship wrecks.
Keep your eyes on the road.

JANUARY 13

READ OUT LOUD: **Philippians 2:3b-4 (NLT)**

Be humble, thinking of others as better than yourselves. Don't look out only for your own interests, but take an interest in others, too.

If you are picky or particular about the way things are done, be careful. Criticism will fill a person with criticism ... for *you*. Ultimately, your life will suffer because you will harvest the pickiness that you have planted.

However, encouragement will fill a person with encouragement ... that *you* will eventually receive. Your life will flourish.

If you see *big* things that need to change, speak in positive terms. Commend more than you confront. Be kind.

If you see *little* things that need to change ... just forget them. At times, the act of forgetting can be a kindness. The little details don't matter compared to how much other people matter.

Pickiness will never endear you to another person.
Be picky at your own risk.

JANUARY 14

READ OUT LOUD: Matthew 7:12a (CJB)

Always treat others as you would like them to treat you.

If you are kind enough to treat someone as if they were *already* a better person, miraculous things will come to pass.

What would happen if you started treating the people who are *not* your favorites, as if they were? What would happen if you invited a cranky colleague to join your lunch group?

You want to be included. Do for others what you want done for you.

Be kind to people, even when they are not kind in return.

This is a beautiful offering to the Lord.

PRAY FOR THE CRANKIEST PERSON YOU KNOW. THEN GO AND DO SOMETHING TO SHOW KINDNESS TO THEM.

_____

_____

_____

_____

_____

_____

JANUARY 15

READ OUT LOUD: Proverbs 31:26 (NLT)

When she speaks, her words are wise, and she gives instructions with kindness.

Think back to when you were a child. If a bite of food were distasteful, you gagged when trying to swallow. And then you gave up, pushing the plate away. It didn't matter that the food was packed with vitamins. It didn't matter that it was good for you. You were too immature to value what was best.

By the same token, some spiritual training from the Lord may be rigorous, but if you find it distasteful, you will push it away. Why would your own children behave differently?

Remember, when it comes to vegetables, there is nothing wrong with glazing the carrots, or topping the sweet potatoes in toasted marshmallows, or tossing candied pecans into the spinach salad.

The one who takes a bite still gets the vitamins.

When you are communicating a concept that is hard for your children to swallow, stir in some sweetness. That is the kind thing to do.

They will still get the vitamins.

And concerning your own spiritual health, start thanking God for the sweetness that He stirs into hard things.

It is always there if you look for it.

JANUARY **16**

READ OUT LOUD: **Proverbs 16:24 (NIV)**

Gracious words are a honeycomb, sweet to the soul and healing to the bones.

There is an interesting story in the Old Testament, when King Saul swears an oath that *no one* in Israel is permitted to eat until their enemies are defeated in battle.

The army is famished. They fight long and hard, becoming weaker with every skirmish. Near the end of the day, the king's son, Jonathan, sees some raw honey as they are walking through the woods.

He eats the honey, and his countenance changes immediately. He says, "My father has made trouble for the country. See how my eyes brightened when I tasted a little of this honey."

Do you catch the connection? Many parents and bosses threaten the way Saul did, saying, "We will have fun when you finish your work!" Don't be like them.

Threats make trouble.
A person's eyes brighten when they taste a little kindness.

JANUARY 17

READ OUT LOUD: 1 Thessalonians 5:11 (NLT)

So encourage each other and build each other up, just as you are already doing.

Encouragement is not something that comes as a reward *after* someone has proven themselves. Encouragement must come *during* the process, while character is still under construction.

How can anyone expect a person to be courageous before they are *encouraged*?

Giving encouragement is one of the kindest things you can do.

USING INITIALS ONLY, PRAY FOR SOMEONE WHO NEEDS ENCOURAGEMENT TODAY.

JANUARY 18

READ OUT LOUD: **Proverbs** 25:11 (NLT)

Timely advice is lovely, like golden apples in a silver basket.

It feels good to have the answer ready on the tip of your tongue.

God knows what people need to hear and when people need to hear it. He can guide you to give timely advice.

Begin your day with a specific prayer about giving timely advice. Place your hand over your mouth and ask God to bless the words that flow from it.

He will help you speak kindly and carefully

WHAT IS THE BEST PIECE OF ADVICE SOMEONE EVER GAVE YOU?

_____

_____

_____

_____

_____

_____

JANUARY **19**

READ OUT LOUD: **Proverbs 15:23 (NLT)**

Everyone enjoys a fitting reply; it is wonderful to say the right thing at the right time!

Giving the right answer feels terrific, but giving the wrong answer feels terrible! Who would risk it?

Remove the fear that public humiliation is a possibility when you are around. Be careful about laughing when someone is teased for a mistake, however small. Even good-natured teasing can get wearisome. When others are teased, let your reaction show that kindness is the expectation.

Others will speak up more if less is at stake.

THANK GOD FOR A PERSON IN YOUR LIFE WHO KNOWS HOW TO SAY THE RIGHT THING AT THE RIGHT TIME.

JANUARY 20

READ OUT LOUD: Colossians 4:6 (NIV)

Let your conversation be always full of grace, seasoned with salt, so that you may know how to answer everyone.

The conversations that you have in the church, office, and home matter a great deal. Just because you close the door so that others will not overhear a conversation, does not mean they will not receive the impact of a conversation.

If you have been speaking negatively as you vent, your family and friends will sense it.

Unkind words leave a stain on your lips.

ASK GOD TO KINDLY AND GENTLY KEEP YOU ACCOUNTABLE FOR THE WORDS THAT YOU SAY.

JANUARY 21

READ OUT LOUD: Luke 4:22a (NLT)

Everyone spoke well of Him and was amazed by the gracious words that came from His lips.

When Jesus taught, His words were extraordinary. He taught with authority.

This is not because He had a stellar vocabulary or elegant diction. He did not have to act as if He were anything other than an ordinary man, a hard worker, a carpenter.

Yes, He was divine, but He never flaunted it.

His words were amazing because they were words like no one had heard before. They were full of kindness and grace, even when He was correcting.

His words convicted people of sin and welcomed them home at the same time.

WHO IS SOMEONE IN YOUR LIFE WHO NEEDS TO BE "WELCOMED HOME?"

_____

_____

JANUARY 22

READ OUT LOUD: 2 Corinthians 9:7 (NIV)

Each of you should give what you have decided in your heart to give, not reluctantly or under compulsion, for God loves a cheerful giver.

Has an opportunity for generosity been rattling around in your thoughts lately? Do you see an area where someone could use a blessing?

Give exactly what is on your heart to give.

God, the Great Giver, is the One who prompts you to be generous. If you obey, He will not let you suffer for it. He will bless you for blessing others.

Your friends and family may never see you give, but they will benefit from being around someone who is kind and generous, just the same.

WRITE A BRIEF PRAYER OF COMMITMENT TO FOLLOW THROUGH WITH GIVING WHAT GOD HAS PUT ON YOUR HEART.

_____

_____

_____

_____

_____

_____

_____

JANUARY 23

READ OUT LOUD: Romans 2:4 (NLT)

Don't you see how wonderfully kind, tolerant, and patient God is with you? Does this mean nothing to you? Can't you see that his kindness is intended to turn you from your sin?

Kindness is the way that God inspires repentance in His children. This should be your pattern.

Kindness will bring about change in others.

Kindness will convict their hearts and turn them around.

Ask the Lord for specific direction when you are faced with someone who stays rebellious.

He knows what that feels like.

USING INITIALS ONLY, PRAY FOR A FRIEND OR FAMILY MEMBER WHO IS IN REBELLION, RUNNING AWAY FROM GOD.

_____

_____

_____

_____

_____

_____

JANUARY 24

READ OUT LOUD: Luke 12:33-34 (MSG)

Be generous. Give to the poor. Get yourselves a bank that can't go bankrupt, a bank in heaven far from bank robbers, safe from embezzlers, a bank you can bank on. It's obvious, isn't it? The place where your treasure is, is the place you will most want to be, and end up being.

Where is a bank that gives you 100% interest? Wouldn't that be nice?

Only God gives a return like that.

He sees every kindness that you extend to others. He sees every dime, every moment of time, you spend. He keeps accurate records in heaven and pours His blessings upon you based on your willingness to share these gifts with others.

Why would He give to someone who plans to hoard it? He has designed blessings to be shared.

That is the Master's multiplication.

REMEMBER A TIME WHEN SOMEONE SHARED THEIR BLESSING WITH YOU.

_____

_____

_____

_____

JANUARY 25

READ OUT LOUD: 2 Corinthians 9:6 (NLT)

Remember this—a farmer who plants only a few seeds will get a small crop. But the one who plants generously will get a generous crop.

Every kindness that leaves your hand will one day find its way back to you, whether at work or at home. This isn't "karma." It is the law of sowing and reaping. Give minimally and you will receive the same.

Plant a lot of seeds if you want a lot of trees.
The bigger the orchard, the bigger the harvest.

THANK GOD FOR FIVE PEOPLE IN YOUR LIFE WHO ARE CONSISTENTLY PLANTING KINDNESS IN THE WORLD.

1. _____
2. _____
3. _____
4. _____
5. _____

JANUARY 26

READ OUT LOUD: **Matthew 6:1 (NKJV)**

Take heed that you do not do your charitable deeds before men, to be seen by them. Otherwise you have no reward from your Father in heaven.

It is tempting to demonstrate kindness in front of others, so that you will be noticed. Instead, be discreet. Do everything you can to offer kindness for the recipient's sake, not for the audience who may be watching.

God will see it and reward you.

The attention you receive from the world will have its limits.

The attention you receive from heaven is everlasting.

LIST THREE KIND THINGS THE LORD IS LEADING YOU TO DO ANONYMOUSLY THIS WEEK.

1. _____
2. _____
3. _____

JANUARY 27

READ OUT LOUD: **Proverbs 3:27 (NIV)**

Do not withhold good from those to whom it is due, when it is in your power to act.

God owns everything on earth, every abundance. He has the power to distribute blessings when and where He wishes.

Think how the world would be different if people viewed *their* belongings as *the Lord's*. They would hold possessions with open hands.

If you give something today, and it leaves a vacuum in your bank account, heart, or life, you can expect God to replace or refill it. It is all His anyway.

Being kind to others will not leave you depleted.

Quite the contrary, it will fill you up.

ASK GOD IF THERE ARE FOUR THINGS HE WOULD LIKE FOR YOU TO GIVE AWAY THIS MONTH.

1. _____
2. _____
3. _____
4. _____

JANUARY 28

READ OUT LOUD: Mark 12:41-44 (MSG)

Sitting across from the offering box, He was observing how the crowd tossed money in for the collection. Many of the rich were making large contributions. One poor widow came up and put in two small coins—a measly two cents. Jesus called His disciples over and said, "The truth is that this poor widow gave more to the collection than all the others put together. All the others gave what they'll never miss; she gave extravagantly what she couldn't afford—she gave her all."

It is not *how much* you give, but *how* you give.

You may feel as if you have little to offer, but small gifts given wholeheartedly have tremendous value.

Jesus stands nearby watching your sacrifice with a smile on His face.

He cannot wait to give back to you every kindness you have given.

HAS THERE EVER BEEN A TIME WHEN SOMEONE GAVE YOU EVERYTHING THEY HAD?

_____

_____

_____

JANUARY 29

READ OUT LOUD: **Proverbs 19:17 (NLT)**

If you help the poor, you are lending to the Lord—and He will repay you!

No matter what neighborhood people live in, they may be experiencing a poverty of kindness.

Let a *smile* be the first thing others receive from you as they enter your presence. Don't make them earn it. Light up when you see them.

Let a warm welcome be their free gift.

LIST THE INITIALS OF THREE PEOPLE WHO NEED EXTRA PRAYER BECAUSE THEIR FAMILIES COULD USE A FINANCIAL BLESSING. ASK GOD TO WORK A MIRACLE ON THEIR BEHALF.

1. _____
2. _____
3. _____

JANUARY 30

READ OUT LOUD: Luke 6:30 (NLT)

Give to anyone who asks; and when things are taken away from you, don't try to get them back.

The wild economy of God says you don't have to defend yourself.

Ask Jesus for the supernatural power to resist retaliation. If someone took something from you without asking, tell them it is your gift to them. Do not insist on having it back.

You serve the Creator of the universe. He has more of everything. Let Him supply and resupply your needs. When you let others take from you, you are not being walked upon as much as you are laying down your life for the One who laid down His life for you...

... and never asked for it back.

USING INITIALS ONLY, PRAY FOR THE PERSON WHO TOOK SOMETHING FROM YOU WITHOUT ASKING. FORGIVE THEM.

JANUARY **31**

READ OUT LOUD: Psalm 16:6 (NIV)

The boundary lines have fallen for me in pleasant places; surely I have a delightful inheritance.

Spiritual gifts are such a kindness from God. They build you and bless you. They build and bless your family.

But to use your spiritual gifts *only* for yourself or *only* for your family is misuse.

Your spiritual gifts are to be extended to bless your community, as well. Open the door of your world and walk through it with the intention to bless, bless, bless everyone you meet.

God has placed you exactly where He wants you.
He put you where people needed kindness.

PRAY A PRAYER OF SURRENDER TO LIVE FULLY WHERE YOU ARE.

FEBRUARY

MEDITATIONS ON GOODNESS

Surely your goodness and unfailing love will pursue me all the days of my life, and I will live in the house of the Lord forever.

Psalm 23:6 (NLT)

FEBRUARY 1

READ OUT LOUD: **Deuteronomy 6:6-7 (NIV)**

These commandments that I give you today are to be on your hearts. Impress them on your children. Talk about them when you sit at home and when you walk along the road, when you lie down and when you get up.

What if God's whispers and actions in your lives became a regular part of what your family talked about at home? How can you inspire the children in your life to talk about the Lord even they are not at church?

De-compartmentalize their experience of Jesus by walking them through a play-by-play of your own day. Ask them to notice all the moments when you discovered His hands at work on your behalf. Show them that following the Lord never really stops. Help them find the bridge between life and church.

Consider directly inviting them to share. Use this convenient conversation starter every now and then: "How have you seen God in your world this week?" For a while, they may roll their eyes and think you're weird for asking. Then, maybe, when you are least expecting it, they will soften their hearts, truly answer the question, and all of heaven will hush to hear it.

Spiritual insight is too good to be left on a pew.
But young people may need some help if they are going to figure out how to take it home.

FEBRUARY 2

READ OUT LOUD: Proverbs 20:7 (MSG)

God-loyal people, living honest lives, make it much easier for their children.

Your goodness paves the way for the generation that comes after you. The future of young people can be blessed by the good decisions you make today.

Your integrity does not go unnoticed. God sees your efforts to do the right thing, and the young people around you see it, too. They may be adults before they are able to articulate what they observe, but their hearts understand it right now.

Seeing a life built upon goodness gives children and teenagers something to imitate. Later, making good choices will feel natural to them because they have watched you do it so many times.

Don't underestimate your impact.
If you live well, they will be more likely to live well.

THANK GOD FOR SOMEONE WHOSE EXAMPLE OF GOOD DECISION-MAKING HAS IMPACTED YOU.

FEBRUARY 3

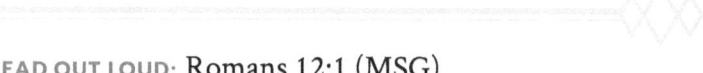

READ OUT LOUD: Romans 12:1 (MSG)

Take your everyday, ordinary life—your sleeping, eating, going-to-work, and walking-around life—and place it before God as an offering. Embracing what God does for you is the best thing you can do for him.

You are a being who is three parts: a spirit, a body, and a soul working together.

You are discovering more and more that your spiritual life—the part of you that connects you to God and gives every word power—can be the invisible ingredient of living well.

Make your connection to Jesus part of your whole life. He will heal any brokenness and give you a *whole* life.

ASK THE LORD TO MAKE YOU WHOLE IN EVERY AREA. ASK HIM TO LEAD YOU TO A HARMONY OF SPIRIT, BODY, AND SOUL, AND OF HEART, HAND, AND MIND.

FEBRUARY 4

READ OUT LOUD: Colossians 3:23 (NIV)

Whatever you do, work at it with all your heart, as working for the Lord, not for human masters.

Your interaction with young people has a lifelong effect on them. Your attitude toward your work will become part of their attitude toward their work.

Emphasize the pleasure of work, both yours and theirs.

When God set Adam and Eve in Eden, He made them gardeners.

He gave them work to do.
And He said it was good.

THANK GOD FOR SIX THINGS ABOUT YOUR WORK THAT ARE GOOD.

1. _____
2. _____
3. _____
4. _____
5. _____
6. _____

FEBRUARY 5

READ OUT LOUD: Proverbs 22:6 (NIV)

Start children off on the way they should go, and even when they are old they will not turn from it.

Have you noticed the cultural trend? More and more young adults do not want to work. Somewhere along the way, the adults in their lives may have leveraged work as discipline, and now they still see work as punitive.

Teach your children that meaningful work is good. Let consequences come from some other place.

LIST FIVE REASONABLE CONSEQUENCES THAT HAVE NOTHING TO DO WITH AN ADDED WORK LOAD FOR YOUR CHILDREN.

1. _____
2. _____
3. _____
4. _____
5. _____

FEBRUARY 6

READ OUT LOUD: **Proverbs 11:3 (NIV)**

The integrity of the upright guides them, but the unfaithful are destroyed by their duplicity.

Why do schools give excellent conduct marks to students who are quiet? Is being *quiet* the mark of good citizenship?

Did you internalize this strange concept when you were growing up? Think about what you do now. Is your occupation one that requires a lot of speaking? Or manual labor? Do you spend your days taking ordinary objects and creating something new? Or do you have a vocation in which you sing or draw?

God placed those desires and skills in you, but you may have gotten in trouble at school for talking too much, for never sitting still, for bending paperclips, or for doodling. It is time we train young people to *use* those attributes appropriately instead of just telling them not to.

There is so much more to goodness than a list of *things not to do.*

WHAT DO YOU THINK IS GOD'S DEFINITION OF A GOOD CITIZEN OF HEAVEN?

_____

_____

_____

FEBRUARY 7

READ OUT LOUD: 1 Peter 3:15b-16 (NIV)

Always be prepared to give an answer to everyone who asks you to give the reason for the hope that you have. But do this with gentleness and respect, keeping a clear conscience, so that those who speak maliciously against your good behavior in Christ may be ashamed of their slander.

What does good citizenship look like ... really?

It looks like respect. Respecting leaders, respecting other citizens, respecting laws, respecting answers, respecting ideas, respecting opinions. Good citizenship is not defined by being quiet.

> Sometimes goodness speaks up.
> But it does so respectfully.

IS THERE AN AREA IN YOUR LIFE WHERE YOU NEED TO SPEAK UP? WRITE A QUICK PRAYER, ASKING GOD TO GIVE YOU COURAGE TO SAY WHAT YOU NEED TO SAY.

FEBRUARY 8

READ OUT LOUD: Psalm 116:15 (NLT)

The Lord cares deeply when His loved ones die.

Your personal emotions affect your professional life. There is no topic more tender than grief. Without comparing the pain-level of different types of loss, you can acknowledge that there is grief involved with all of them.

One of the things that is essential for healthy grieving is *talk*. Talking can be a goodness to your heart. Process grief by talking about it, even when those around you have stopped talking about it.

Talk to God.

Talk to a counselor.

Talk to a friend.

And don't be afraid to talk about pain with children. Young people lose pets, grandparents, and others. They are confused if no one ever talks about grief and loss. It is all right to let them know that sometimes your heart hurts, too.

Young people need to know that it is good to talk about grief.

Loss may involve a burial, but pain should never be buried.

FEBRUARY 9

READ OUT LOUD: John 10:10b (NLT)

My purpose is to give them a rich and satisfying life.

At work, you may be feeling superficial. You try to keep a smile on your face in front of your employer and colleagues, but when you are hurting, smiling may be difficult.

Even if your soul is numb, ask God for help so that it won't stay that way indefinitely. Do you feel that way because a dream or desire has died?

> Ask your good God for a resurrection.
> It's what the Author of Life loves to do.

ASK GOD IF THERE IS SOMETHING YOU THINK IS LONG GONE—AN IDEA, HOBBY, PLAN, DREAM, OR DESIRE—THAT HE WANTS TO BRING BACK TO LIFE. WRITE DOWN WHAT HE TELLS YOU.

FEBRUARY 10

READ OUT LOUD: John 1:4-5 (NLT)

The Word gave life to everything that was created, and his life brought light to everyone. The light shines in the darkness, and the darkness can never extinguish it.

There are many things that fall into the category of darkness: depression, grief, sorrow, bitterness, hurt, and all kinds of brokenness.

This is why Jesus had to come for you. This is why He is coming again. In the meantime, He left the Holy Spirit and Scripture as your weapons for the fight.

Defeat darkness with the power of goodness. Apply the Word to yourself. Apply it to your family and friends.

Some people may see progress faster than others when they reach for Scripture daily, reading it aloud and meditating on it. You are in a spiritual war. Do not expect all battles to be fought in the same time frame. Some take longer than others.

But Jesus wins every last one of them.
Take the sword of His Word into combat.

LOOK FOR A BIBLE VERSE YOU CAN TAKE INTO YOUR CURRENT BATTLE. WRITE IT HERE.

_____

_____

_____

FEBRUARY 11

READ OUT LOUD: **Galatians 3:3 (CJB)**

Are you that stupid? Having begun with the Spirit's power, do you think you can reach the goal under your own power?

Perfection only *seems* like goodness.

People who are obsessed with perfection may be locked away from God's power. And the whole time, they think perfection is what God expects.

But God gives His overcoming power to those who know they need it, not to those who act like they don't.

Perfection draws people to look at you, not Him. Honor God by pointing others to *His* image, not your own.

> Your Heavenly Father is good.
> Seek reflection, not perfection.

LORD, I SURRENDER THE AREA OF _____ TODAY. MY EFFORTS ARE NOT ENOUGH WITHOUT YOU. PLEASE TAKE MY IMPERFECTIONS AND MAKE THEM REFLECTIONS OF YOUR GOODNESS.

FEBRUARY 12

READ OUT LOUD: **Proverbs 25:2a (NIV)**

It is the glory of God to conceal a matter.

You are meant for mystery. God does not want to keep you in the dark, but He delights in revealing things according to His design.

You wouldn't like it if your children were constantly trying to peer into a birthday present where you had hidden a surprise for them. It would be even worse if they reached for what you were holding behind your back, trying to take it from your hands. In the same way, don't take gifts out of God's hands too soon. Let Him place them in yours at just the right time.

God isn't going to withhold goodness from you.
His perfect timing is the *real* goodness.

IF GOD IS NUDGING YOUR HEART THAT YOU HAVE TAKEN SOMETHING OUT OF HIS HANDS TOO SOON, PRAY AND TRY TO ENVISION YOURSELF PUTTING IT BACK INTO HIS PALM.

FEBRUARY 13

READ OUT LOUD: James 4:17 (NLT)

Remember, it is sin to know what you ought to do and then not do it.

Sometimes God gives more challenging tasks to experienced believers.

God is just and right in all that He does. If He communicates different expectations to different people, you can trust that His assignments are distributed fairly.

Do what He asks of you. A blessing awaits those who learn this.

Obedience is not about your goodness.
It is about responding to *God's* goodness.

ASK GOD FOR STRENGTH TO OBEY.

FEBRUARY 14

READ OUT LOUD: Ephesians 2:8-9 (NLT)

God saved you by his grace when you believed. And you can't take credit for this; it is a gift from God. Salvation is not a reward for the good things we have done, so none of us can boast about it.

When the Lord moves your heart to do good things or act in good ways, it is never so that you can earn something from Him. A good life doesn't earn His love.

Think of someone you care about. Do you love them for the good things they do? No, your love is a free gift. But when they respond to your love by doing good things, you want to do good things for them in return.

It is a cycle of goodness.

This is an oversimplified way of looking at God's cycle of goodness. He loves you, and so you do good things as a response, not as a requirement.

On this special day that represents love, remind those around you that your love for them is unconditional.

And they don't have to earn it.

ASK GOD TO HELP YOU LOVE LIKE HE DOES.

FEBRUARY 15

READ OUT LOUD: **Hebrews 13:16 (NIV)**

And do not forget to do good and to share with others, for with such sacrifices God is pleased.

The rhythm of God's good Kingdom is counter-cultural.

To live, you must die to yourself.

To have all you need, you must give it away.

God defines goodness as service. The more a leader chooses to serve in humility, the more He is like God. Jesus, the King of all kings, made Himself low and washed His disciples' feet.

God is pleased when we serve because we look so much like Him. Every father enjoys seeing his mannerisms and likeness in his children.

Think of ways to serve your friends, your relative, and your workplace.

Keep God's family resemblance strong.

WRITE TWO AREAS WHERE YOU NEED GOD TO GIVE YOU GRACE TO BE ESPECIALLY GOOD AND SERVE SOMEONE WHO NEEDS IT.

1. _____

2. _____

FEBRUARY 16

READ OUT LOUD: Titus 2:7 (NLT)

And you yourself must be an example to them by doing good works of every kind. Let everything you do reflect the integrity and seriousness of your teaching.

Don't forget that you are always on a stage. People are watching you everywhere. They see the way you speak to people at lunch, in the gym, at the office, and on the phone.

Modeling is the most effective type of evangelizing. If you give your people a glimpse of Jesus, they may want to get to know Him better.

Be consistent.
Who you are will reinforce *what you do.*

ASK GOD IF THERE IS ONE AREA IN YOUR LIFE WHERE HE WANTS YOU TO STOP DIRECTLY MINISTERING AND START INDIRECTLY MODELING WHAT YOU BELIEVE. WRITE DOWN WHAT HE SAYS.

FEBRUARY **17**

READ OUT LOUD: Psalm 31:19 (NLT)

How great is the goodness you have stored up for those who fear you. You lavish it on those who come to you for protection, blessing them before the watching world.

It speaks well of God when His people trust Him publicly. God loves to hear you say that you trust Him to take care of everything.

Things may get worse before they get better. This is one way to cement your trust in Him. Shallow waters deepen in a storm, and so does your faith. The louder the winds become, the more people will want to see what keeps you anchored.

God has never let any of His followers fall out of His hands. He knows what He is doing, and He gives generously in response to public faith. He keeps an ample supply of goodness in a storehouse, saved as a reward for those who live out what they believe.

You will not fail at this. In fact, God is already planning for your success.

You do the same thing, don't you? You plan for your children's success or your employees' success, by keeping a few ideas in the back of your mind to show your appreciation. Your desire to reward comes from God.

He taught you how to expect success in others.
He is expecting yours.

FEBRUARY 18

READ OUT LOUD: Psalm 145:15-19 (NLT)

The eyes of all look to you in hope; you give them their food as they need it. When you open your hand, you satisfy the hunger and thirst of every living thing. The Lord is righteous in everything he does; he is filled with kindness. The Lord is close to all who call on him, yes, to all who call on him in truth. He grants the desires of those who fear him; he hears their cries for help and rescues them.

The verse above is so rich, that to add a devotional thought to it would be like pouring sugar on a dessert that is already perfect: it would spoil a good thing.

Savor the sweetness.
Read it again.

THANK THE LORD FOR THE STUNNING TRUTHS MENTIONED IN THE VERSE ABOVE.

FEBRUARY 19

READ OUT LOUD: **Romans 12:9a (NKJV)**

Let love be without hypocrisy. Abhor what is evil. Cling to what is good.

You may not like this, but the moment someone hears you are a Christian, they start watching you with different eyes. They begin looking for areas where you will mess up.

This is not fair, but it happens.

People find it hard to believe that God is really good. They find it harder to believe that His followers are really good.

Carefully consider the media you bring into your life. Other people, especially young people, are noticing the music you allow to fill your ears and the movies you allow to fill your eyes. More than that, they are paying attention to the words you allow to fill your mouth.

> Deliberately use speech that is uplifting.
> Intentionally choose goodness.

ASK GOD TO HELP YOU IMPROVE YOUR VOCABULARY.

FEBRUARY 20

READ OUT LOUD: Psalm 27:13 (NKJV)

I would have lost heart, unless I had believed that I would see the goodness of the Lord in the land of the living.

Belief is the glue that attaches blessing to your life.
Without belief, blessing might come, but it won't stay.

STOP AND GET ON YOUR KNEES FOR A MOMENT, IF YOU CAN. LET THAT POSTURE BE A PHYSICAL SYMBOL OF YOUR SPIRITUAL SUBMISSION. PRAY AND RECOMMIT TO BELIEVE WHAT GOD HAS SAID.

FEBRUARY 21

READ OUT LOUD: James 1:17 (NIV)

Every good and perfect gift is from above, coming down from the Father of the heavenly lights, who does not change like shifting shadows.

The same God who parted the Red Sea for the Israelites is able to prepare the way before you.

The same God who multiplied loaves and fish to feed five thousand people is able to provide for you.

The same God who kept the Ten Plagues from touching the Israelites is able to protect you.

Preparation, provision, and protection. He sends these good gifts to His followers.

He always has and He always will.

SOME PREPARATION I HAVE SEEN IN MY LIFE: _____

_____

_____

SOME PROVISION I HAVE SEEN IN MY LIFE: _____

_____

_____

SOME PROTECTION I HAVE SEEN IN MY LIFE: _____

_____

_____

FEBRUARY 22

READ OUT LOUD: Micah 6:8 (NIV)

He has shown you, O mortal, what is good. And what does the Lord require of you? To act justly and to love mercy and to walk humbly with your God.

Make the list of expectations for those you love short and simple. The longer the series of requirements, the less a person connects.

God's expectations of you can be summed up on a short and simple list:

Justice.
Mercy.
Humility.

If the choices you make illustrate those three values, then they will be good choices indeed.

Give others freedom, the way God has given freedom to you.

CHOOSE THREE DRIVING VALUES FOR YOUR RELATIONSHIPS. ALLOW PEOPLE TO CHOOSE HOW THEY ILLUSTRATE THOSE VALUES.

1. _____
2. _____
3. _____

FEBRUARY 23

READ OUT LOUD: Galatians 6:15-16 (NLT)

What counts is whether we have been transformed into a new creation. May God's peace and mercy be upon all who live by this principle; they are the new people of God.

It is easy to be caught in the current of reports and evaluation in our world. It's all about measurement. People want growth that can be counted.

Don't second-guess your efforts and effectiveness when you don't measure up to the standard arbitrarily set for you.

Ask yourself this question: Would it be a good year if you met a goal, but did not grow in character? If you didn't value integrity? If you didn't pursue goodness?

Evaluate your performance by different standards. Seek to motivate real transformation in yourself, real growth. As you become better at being a reflection of Christ, other successes will be an indirect result.

The measure of character may not be something you can count, but it is what counts most.

FEBRUARY 24

READ OUT LOUD: Isaiah 38:16 (NLT)

Lord, your discipline is good, for it leads to life and health.
You restore my health and allow me to live!

Your human mind cannot determine what is good.

You think what is comfortable or easy or pleasing is good.

But God knows anything that brings you closer to Him and to the center of His will is good.

There is nothing about discipline that is comfortable or easy or pleasing. There are times, however, when God's blessing takes the form of discipline. Discipline means that He loves you. He wants you to become more like Him every day. He wants you to become more like the person you were designed to be.

Discipline, when administered out of love, is good. Receive loving discipline from the Lord.

It will bring goodness that you cannot get any other way.

THANK GOD FOR SOMETHING THAT DIDN'T FEEL GOOD AT THE TIME, BUT HAS BECOME A BLESSING.

_____

_____

_____

FEBRUARY 25

READ OUT LOUD: Psalm 23:6 (NLT)

Surely your goodness and unfailing love will pursue me all the days of my life, and I will live in the house of the Lord forever.

Think of that old Looney Tunes cartoon in which the big tough dog, Spike, walks silently along the sidewalk while the smaller, yapping dog tries to get his attention. The small dog, Chester, jumps across Spike's back—excitedly talking on his left side, jump, talking on his right side, jump...

You wanna play ball, Spike? Huh, Spike? You wanna chase cars, Spike? Huh, Spike, huh?

Spike smacks Chester away with one blow and keeps on walking. But Chester doesn't quit. He comes running back, and keeps trying to get Spike's attention.

He tries again. *You wanna beat up a cat, Spike?*

Spike stops in his tracks, fully engaged. "A cat?" the big dog says. Chester has finally found the key to Spike's interest.

Consider ways to pursue someone God brings to mind today. That person may smack you away from time to time, but goodness won't give up the chase.

Keep following them until you find the key to their interests.

For then you will have found the key to their hearts.

FEBRUARY 26

READ OUT LOUD: Romans 12:9a (MSG)

Love from the center of who you are; don't fake it. Run for dear life from evil; hold on for dear life to good.

There is a way you can adopt this practice in your thoughts.

Whenever you discover something negative about anyone—and it is going to happen eventually—decide that you will not dwell on that aspect of their lives.

When you have an irritating or critical thought about someone, immediately follow that with two good or grateful thoughts about that person. Then let that be where your thoughts dwell.

If you cannot find two good things about someone, it might indicate a problem with *you* more than them. You are made in God's image, and if there is one thing that God does well, it is finding the good in people. You were designed to do the same thing.

You can choose where you let your thoughts live.
Make sure your mind is a good neighborhood.

LIST TWO GOOD QUALITIES IN A PERSON WHO SOMETIMES IRRITATES YOU.

1. _____

2. _____

FEBRUARY 27

READ OUT LOUD: Psalm 34:8 (NLT)

Taste and see that the Lord is good. Oh, the joys of those who take refuge in him!

The only way to know if God is good is to taste and see. One sweet quality of the Fruit of the Spirit is goodness.

And it will grow in you when you abide in the Vine. Give it time.

TAKE A MOMENT TO EXPRESS YOUR GRATITUDE TO JESUS FOR THE WAYS HE IS GROWING GOODNESS IN YOU.

___

___

___

___

___

___

___

FEBRUARY 28

READ OUT LOUD: **Matthew 12:35 (NLT)**

A good man brings good things out of the good stored up in him, and an evil man brings evil things out of the evil stored up in him.

When you are commuting to work, what are you feeding your mind? How are you nourishing your heart? Are you preparing for the tasks you will meet when you arrive?

Drive-time is prime-time. Maybe what interests you needs to take a backseat to what inspires you.

You have a choice about what you welcome into your heart and mind right now. But later, in times of stress, you may not have a choice about what comes out.

Squeeze a sponge, and it releases everything it has soaked up.

ASK GOD IF THERE IS SOMETHING HE WOULD LIKE YOU TO STOP SOAKING UP.

FEBRUARY 29

READ OUT LOUD: Psalm 84:11b (NLT)

The Lord will withhold no good thing from those who do what is right.

Your highest goal should be to show your others the character of Jesus. That standard supersedes every other.

One way you can live like Him is to make goodness a valued characteristic within you.

Walk out the door every morning with the intention to bless someone.

Look for people who are trying to do what is right and commend them.

Keep uplifting words ready to share.

It is a thrilling cycle: When you withhold no good thing from others, God withholds no good thing from you.

Jesus is *your* Great Example.

You don't have to speak His name to live in His name.

ASK JESUS TO MAKE YOU LOOK MORE LIKE HIM.

MARCH

MEDITATIONS ON FAITHFULNESS

If we are faithless, he remains faithful, for he cannot disown himself.

2 Timothy 2:13 (NIV)

MARCH 1

READ OUT LOUD: Psalm 89:33 (NIV)

I will not take my love from him, nor will I ever betray my faithfulness.

Jesus is faithful.

He has never betrayed you, no matter who else has.

He has never left your side, no matter who else has.

He has never told you a lie, no matter who else has.

He has never broken a promise to you, no matter who else has.

He has never given up on you, no matter who else has.

He has never stopped loving you, no matter who else has.

He has never stopped providing for you, no matter who else has.

And He is strong enough to love you, no matter what.

Do you feel heavy with all you are longing for? Remember His faithfulness.

You can put all your weight on Him.
You can put all your *wait* on Him.

MARCH 2

READ OUT LOUD: Psalm 91:4 (NIV)

He will cover you with his feathers, and under his wings you will find refuge; his faithfulness will be your shield and rampart.

In John 6, Jesus asks His disciples, "You don't want to leave, do you?"

Peter answers wholeheartedly, "Where else would we go?"

Find refuge in the One who is faithful to you.
Where else would you go?

WHEN YOU DESCRIBE GOD AS A REFUGE, WHAT IMAGE COMES TO MIND? WHAT IS A REFUGE TO YOU?

MARCH 3

READ OUT LOUD: 2 Timothy 2:13 (NIV)

... if we are faithless, he remains faithful, for he cannot disown himself.

God has always loved you.

He loves you now.

He will always love you.

He knows how to love longer and better than anyone. No one can comprehend His faithful love.

When your schedule becomes demanding, He loves you anyway. When daily distractions take your attention away from Him, He loves you anyway.

A day turns into a week, a week turns into a month, a month turns into several months, and finally you sense the distance you have created between you and your Creator. You feel guilty. You wonder if His feelings have changed.

But ...

Love is not what God *does*.

Love is not what God *feels*.

Love is what God *is*, and He never changes.

Even if you have.

He is waiting for you right where He's always been. And He is not going anywhere.

MARCH 4

READ OUT LOUD: **Proverbs 20:6 (CJB)**

Most people announce that they show kindness, but who can find someone faithful [enough to do it]?

It takes the shine off of a gesture to talk about how you are *going to* do it.

Just do it.
Faithfulness does its walking without talking.

LIST TWO THINGS YOU ARE GOING TO FOCUS ON *DOING* INSTEAD OF *TALKING ABOUT* FOR A WHILE.

1. _____
2. _____

MARCH 5

READ OUT LOUD: **Proverbs 3:3 (NIV)**

Let love and faithfulness never leave you; bind them around your neck, write them on the tablet of your heart.

God's timing is perfect.

Write that on your heart.

You would want God's great design if you could see all the way to the finish line. Until then, focus your wait on your faithful God.

Do you find yourself constantly looking at the time, wishing it away? Are you afraid too much time is passing as you hope for your promise?

Have you become like a student who is staring at the clock on the wall, waiting for the last bell to ring?

The lesson isn't over, yet.

Turn your eyes toward your Teacher.

WRITE ABOUT ONE THING YOU HAVE LEARNED DURING THE WAIT.

_____

_____

_____

_____

_____

_____

MARCH 6

READ OUT LOUD: Hebrews 11:1 (NIV)

Now faith is confidence in what we hope for and assurance about what we do not see.

May you wake up with a new song every morning

May you sing it in the grocery store, while sitting at a red light, as you wash the dishes, and when you are working in the yard.

May you smile for no reason.

May your spirit be light.

May you feel the pleasure of waiting on a faithful God.

You don't have to *see* the answers to your prayers to live like they are on their way.

THANK GOD FOR FIVE PEOPLE, PLACES, OR THINGS THAT MAKE YOU SMILE FOR NO REASON.

1. _____
2. _____
3. _____
4. _____
5. _____

MARCH 7

READ OUT LOUD: **2 Peter 3:9 (NIV)**

The Lord is not slow in keeping his promise, as some understand slowness.

If God has spoken to you about something, know that He never wastes His breath.

You can wait in confidence. It may take longer than you expect, but try not to become impatient.

Think about how children often miscalculate the passage of time. When they have been waiting for a few minutes, they say they have been waiting *forever*.

Recognize that what feels like a long time to you is only a moment to your Father. And if He asks you to wait, it is for your good.

You are not waiting because He has forgotten you.
You are waiting because He is faithful to you.

THANK GOD FOR THE WAIT.

MARCH 8

READ OUT LOUD: Hebrews 11:6 (MSG)

Anyone who wants to approach God must believe both that he exists and *that he cares enough to respond to those who seek him.*

Don't waste time praying mild prayers.

Pray the kind of wild prayers that honor God for who He is.

Pray like you know He has absolute power.

Pray like you know He is absolutely faithful

Persistently ask.
Expect to receive.
Persistently seek.
Expect to find.
Persistently knock.
Expect to walk through open doors.

LIST THREE WILD PRAYERS YOU ARE GOING TO KEEP PRAYING.

1. _____
2. _____
3. _____

MARCH 9

READ OUT LOUD: Isaiah 30:18 (CJB)

Yet Adonai is just waiting to show you favor, he will have pity on you from on high; for Adonai is a God of justice; happy are all who wait for him!

God is waiting to show you favor.

He invites you to come to Him with a submitted heart and the desire to partner with Him. He hopes to pour out the surprises and blessings He has in store for you.

He is faithfully listening for your footsteps.

He says, "Make the slightest move toward Me, and I will run to you. We won't have to meet in the middle. I will cover the distance between us and be there by your side in a flash."

Knowing that this is God's attitude toward you, convey the same attitude toward others. Try to avoid a demeanor that expects an equal compromise, meeting in the middle.

Faithfulness goes the extra mile.

Invite others to come to you, and get ready to run to them.

CLOSE YOUR EYES AND IMAGINE YOURSELF COMING HOME AFTER A LONG JOURNEY. PICTURE JESUS RUNNING AS FAST AS HE CAN TO SCOOP YOUR TIRED BODY INTO HIS ARMS AND CARRY YOU THE REST OF THE WAY.

MARCH 10

READ OUT LOUD: Philippians 1:6 (NLT)

And I am certain that God, who began the good work within you, will continue his work until it is finally finished on the day when Christ Jesus returns.

The Faithful Gardener has planted good seeds in you. He does not want them to stay buried. He longs for His best to grow. He has envisioned a stunning landscape of abundance in your life.

Time with you is how He brings blessings to bloom.

THANK THE LORD FOR THREE THINGS THAT ARE BEGINNING TO BLOOM IN YOUR LIFE.

1. _____
2. _____
3. _____

MARCH **11**

READ OUT LOUD: **Malachi 3:6 (NLT)**

I am the Lord, and I do not change.

It is easy to fall prey to frustration at this point in the year. Your goals may not be exactly where you had hoped they would be, but you can combat discouragement by focusing on what has happened, not on what *hasn't*.

You are a mighty warrior. God has empowered and equipped you for your heavenly assignment. He will be with you to see it through.

Just as He helped Noah and Abraham and Moses and Joshua and many others, He will help you. He was faithful to them and He will be faithful to you.

Times may have changed since the Bible was written, but God hasn't.

TAKE A MOMENT TO REFLECT. MAKE NOTE OF THE WONDERFUL THINGS THAT HAVE ALREADY HAPPENED THIS YEAR.

_____

_____

_____

_____

_____

_____

MARCH 12

READ OUT LOUD: Hosea 2:20 (NLT)

I will be faithful to you and make you mine, and you will finally know me as the Lord.

God is a faithful Father to you. Thank Him for the gifts He faithfully gives. And then give Him a gift in return.

Do you know what He really wants?

He wants your concerns.

Bring Him your needs again and again over the coming weeks. Wrap your worries in gratitude and tie them up with a satin bow of trust.

Give them to God like gifts.

Nobody on earth would want to receive a great, big package of anxiety, but God wants that from you. When you offer it to Him, He takes it with a smile.

Put prayer in His hands like a present.

Everything on your heart is His favorite thing to receive.

LIST THE TOP FIVE CONCERNS YOU ARE GIVING TO JESUS TODAY.

1. _____
2. _____
3. _____
4. _____
5. _____

MARCH 13

READ OUT LOUD: Exodus 34:6-7 (NIV)

The Lord, the Lord, the compassionate and gracious God, slow to anger, abounding in love and faithfulness, maintaining love to thousands, and forgiving wickedness, rebellion and sin.

God demonstrates His faithfulness by being slow to anger. Even when He has a good reason to get angry, He is slow...
to...
anger.

ASK GOD TO HELP YOU IN THE AREA OF ANGER. NO NEED TO EXPLAIN IT. JUST ASK FOR HELP.

MARCH 14

READ OUT LOUD: Joshua 24:14 (NIV)

Now fear the Lord and serve him with all faithfulness.

It is one thing to serve, and it is another to serve with *all faithfulness*.

What are some words that are synonymous with *all faithfulness*? What makes the difference between serving or serving with *all faithfulness* to you?

FINISH THIS SENTENCE—

NOW FEAR THE LORD AND SERVE HIM WITH:

1. _____
2. _____
3. _____
4. _____
5. _____

MARCH 15

READ OUT LOUD: Psalm 25:10 (NLT)

The Lord leads with unfailing love and faithfulness all who keep his covenant and obey his demands.

Faithfulness comes in many forms. Different people receive it in different ways.

Today, look for *one* person who needs to receive faithfulness through your **words**.

- Give someone a spoken affirmation.
- Offer someone a vote of confidence.
- Tell someone an encouragement to keep going.

MARCH 16

READ OUT LOUD: Psalm 36:5 (NKJV)

Your mercy, O Lord, is in the heavens; Your faithfulness reaches to the clouds.

Faithfulness comes in many forms. Different people receive it in different ways.

Today, look for *one* person who needs to receive faithfulness through your **touch**.

- Give someone an unexpected hug.
- Offer someone a pat on the back.
- Extend a handshake to someone.

MARCH 17

READ OUT LOUD: Psalm 37:3 (NKJV)

Trust in the Lord, and do good; Dwell in the land, and feed on His faithfulness.

Faithfulness comes in many forms. Different people receive it in different ways.

Today, look for *one* person who needs to receive faithfulness through your **assistance**.

- Carry something for someone.
- Give someone an offer of 2-3 hours of help on their big project.
- Serve someone in a small, practical way by mowing their yard or bringing their family dinner.

MARCH 18

READ OUT LOUD: Isaiah 38:19b (NLT)

Each generation tells of your faithfulness to the next.

Faithfulness comes in many forms. Different people receive it in different ways.

Today, look for *one* person who needs to receive faithfulness through your **nearness**.

- Sit a little closer to a family member than you usually do.
- Ask a friend who lives a good distance away if they would be willing to meet in the middle for lunch. Or offer to go the extra distance and drive to them.
- Call someone and say, "I just wanted to call to let you know I'm *here* for you." See what happens next.

MARCH **19**

READ OUT LOUD: Isaiah 25:1 (NIV)

Lord, you are my God; I will exalt you and praise your name, for in perfect faithfulness you have done wonderful things, things planned long ago.

Faithfulness comes in many forms. Different people receive it in different ways.

Today, look for *one* person who needs to receive faithfulness through your **thoughtfulness**.

- Text a cartoon or meme you thought would make someone laugh.
- Grab a small treat to give them, just because: a pack of gum or some candy or a soft drink. Choose something they have mentioned or you have seen them use.
- Invite them over for dinner and tell them you want to cook (or order in) their favorite meal.

MARCH 20

READ OUT LOUD: Joel 2:23 (NLT)

For the rain he sends demonstrates his faithfulness. Once more the autumn rains will come, as well as the rains of spring.

Sometimes you are too hard on yourself for your mistakes.

Don't worry. Just start over and be faithful to God, knowing He will be faithful to you. He can take your mistakes and turn them into something that serves the bigger purpose. A mistake has never stopped Him.

Your failures will never have the lasting impact of your faithfulness.

MAKE A LIST OF THE PEOPLE WHO HAVE MADE A LASTING IMPACT ON YOUR LIFE BY BEING FAITHFUL TO YOU.

1. _____
2. _____
3. _____
4. _____
5. _____

MARCH 21

READ OUT LOUD: Deuteronomy 4:4 (NLT)

But all of you who were faithful to the Lord your God are still alive today—every one of you.

You can easily remember someone who exhibited faithfulness, even if they are no longer a part of your life.

Faithfulness leaves an impression like nothing else. In a sense, it lives forever.

Your example of daily faithfulness will live on long after they leave this earth. That should be an enormous comfort to you.

Your influence will last forever.

The ripple effect of a faithful person has a life of its own.

LIST FIVE AREAS WHERE YOU NEED GOD'S GRACE TO BE FAITHFUL.

1. _____
2. _____
3. _____
4. _____
5. _____

MARCH 22

READ OUT LOUD: Genesis 39:21 (NLT)

But the Lord was with Joseph in the prison and showed him His faithful love. And the Lord made Joseph a favorite with the prison warder.

Just because someone tells you *no* here on earth does not mean that God is saying *no* in heaven. He might be guiding you to a completely different *yes*.

He also might be wanting you to pray through the *no* until you see it changing into His *yes* for you.

Remember that Joseph faced many earthly *no*'s, from being thrown in a pit by his family to being thrown in prison by his employer. But none of his earthly *no*'s stayed a *no*. Eventually, every one of them became a heavenly *yes*, and he was promoted to second in command of Egypt.

God had the final say.

Your *yes* might be in a completely different direction. And it also might be straight ahead, on the other side of that *no*.

If you are up against a *no*, maybe you need to keep going.

Pray through for breakthrough.

MARCH 23

READ OUT LOUD: Hebrews 13:7-8 (MSG)

Take a good look at the way [your leaders] live, and let their faithfulness instruct you, as well as their truthfulness. There should be a consistency that runs through us all. For Jesus doesn't change—yesterday, today, tomorrow, He's always totally himself.

The Lord accepts all kinds of worthless trade-ins in return for valuable upgrades.

He trades your fear for His peace.

He trades your anger for His forgiveness for others.

He trades your grief for His comfort.

He trades your rejection for His acceptance.

Anything you surrender will be swapped out for something better: your true identity in Him.

This is what it means to *be yourself*.

You are designed to be peaceful, forgiving, comforting, accepting, and fully present to others.

When you receive those things from Christ, you are able to *be* those things to the people in your life, including yourself.

MARCH **24**

READ OUT LOUD: Ephesians 3:12 (CJB)

In union with him, through his faithfulness, we have boldness and confidence when we approach God.

Approach God boldly. He has been expecting you. He has prepared a seat for you. You will find a place card with your name on it.

Remember the last time you planned a party or dinner and prepared in eager expectation for your guests? You knew their names and you knew your plans for the evening and you waited.

What if they hadn't come?

God has given you an invitation to ask Him for guidance. He will not force your path, but if you ask Him, He will show you the best one to take each day.

If you want or need direction, if you're wondering where to go, sit down at the table He has prepared for you and have a conversation with Him. Ask the Lord for His input in your life. He may show you the answer today or He may show you later, but He will show you. Go to the seat with your name on it. He has been waiting for you to come.

MAKE AN APPOINTMENT FOR SOME EXTENDED TIME ALONE WITH GOD.

DAY:_____

TIME:_____

MARCH 25

READ OUT LOUD: **Deuteronomy 32:4 (NIV)**

He is the Rock; his deeds are perfect. Everything he does is just and fair. He is a faithful God who does no wrong; how just and upright is he!

A common complaint in the workplace is that a boss is being unfair.

It may not be true. Some employers would be hurt by this accusation because they know how often they go out of their way to be just and fair.

Being called *unfair* is an insult.

God has gone out of His way to be just and fair with all of His children. If you think He is being unfair, that is an accusation He doesn't deserve.

It is an insult.
And it hurts Him just as it would you.

IF YOU HAVE ACCUSED GOD OF BEING UNFAIR, TAKE A MOMENT TO APOLOGIZE.

MARCH 26

READ OUT LOUD: Lamentations 3:23 (NLT)

Great is His faithfulness; his mercies begin afresh each morning.

Every relationship is perfect ... before it begins.
Every year is perfect ... before it begins.
A faithful person extends renewing mercy within an imperfect relationship.
A faithful person extends renewing mercy within an imperfect year.

Faithfulness focuses on giving, not receiving.
If you are willing to overlook flaws, you will find beauty.

NOTICE AND NAME BEAUTY THAT CAN BE FOUND IN THREE AREAS WHERE YOU USUALLY SEE ONLY FLAWS.

1. _____
2. _____
3. _____

MARCH 27

READ OUT LOUD: Psalm 51:6 (NIV)

Yet you desired faithfulness even in the womb; you taught me wisdom in that secret place.

God is able to keep you from making mistakes, but He is also able to redeem the mistakes you have already made.

He will give you what it takes to live faithfully. Never fear that you will fail. You are made in the image of God, and because the fabric of His being is unfailing faithfulness, it is also the fabric of *your* being.

You may slip and fall, of course, but you will get back up because you know who you are.

It is not in your nature to give up.
You are made to be faithful, like your Father.

THANK GOD FOR A PERSON IN YOUR LIFE WHO IS AN EXAMPLE OF NEVER GIVING UP.

MARCH 28

READ OUT LOUD: Psalm 57:9-10 (MSG)

I'm thanking you, God, out loud in the streets, singing your praises in town and country. The deeper your love, the higher it goes; every cloud is a flag to your faithfulness.

Think about approaching a traffic jam on the highway, one that gives you a feeling of dread when you roll to a stop.

You look ahead and notice a familiar exit sign. You consider taking the exit because you know all the back roads to get where you are going.

But shortcuts don't always get you there any faster.

If you are waiting for God to move, decide to wait actively instead of passively. There are ways you can use this time well. Do not "exit the highway" just yet. Make the most of your time waiting.

Let God get you where you need to go.
Stay the course.

LIST FOUR THINGS YOU CAN DO TO MAKE THE MOST OF YOUR TIME WAITING.

1. _____
2. _____
3. _____
4. _____

MARCH 29

READ OUT LOUD: **Proverbs 20:28 (NLT)**

Unfailing love and faithfulness protect the king; his throne is made secure through love.

You protect your influence when you demonstrate faithfulness.

Do you sense a loyalty problem somewhere in your life? Have people talked disrespectfully to you or gossiped behind your back? Do you sense one or two stirring trouble against you?

Respond to them with the very thing that you are wanting them to give to you: faithfulness.

Show them loyalty in return for their unkindness.
Love may be the very thing that secures your position.

USING INITIALS ONLY, PRAY FOR AND BLESS A PERSON WHO MAY HAVE TURNED HIS BACK ON YOU.

MARCH 30

READ OUT LOUD: Psalm 86:11 (NIV)

Teach me your way, Lord, that I may rely on your faithfulness; give me an undivided heart, that I may fear your name.

God wants you to be like Him.

God is Love.

He is not half-hearted love, not part-time love, not the kind of love you may have known in the past.

When He offers to give you an undivided heart, He means that He will teach you how to love and live wholeheartedly.

WHAT WOULD GOD SAY IT MEANS TO LIVE WHOLEHEARTEDLY?

_____
_____
_____
_____
_____
_____
_____

MARCH 31

READ OUT LOUD: Psalm 85:11 (NIV)

Love and faithfulness meet together; righteousness and peace kiss each other.

Faithfulness is Love's identical twin.

What does *Love* look like as the giver gives it?

Faithfulness.

What does *Faithfulness* look like as the recipient receives it?

Love.

THANK GOD FOR THREE PEOPLE WHO TAUGHT YOU HOW TO LOVE.

1. _____
2. _____
3. _____

APRIL

MEDITATIONS ON GENTLENESS

You have also given me the shield of Your salvation; Your gentleness has made me great.

2 Samuel 22:36 (NKJV)

APRIL 1

READ OUT LOUD: Titus 3:1-2 (CJB)

> *Remind people to submit to the government and its officials, to obey them, to be ready to do any honorable kind of work, to slander no one, to avoid quarrelling, to be friendly, and to behave gently towards everyone.*

Blessing will come to you if you align yourself with the authority that God has placed over you.

Jesus is gentle. When you serve, speak, and submit with gentleness, it provides an opportunity for Jesus' voice to be heard and His face to be seen. Be gentle when you communicate with those in authority in your life.

Gentleness is the mother-tongue of respect.

It will unlock people's hearts, and help them understand what you are saying in a new and meaningful way.

THANK THE LORD FOR THREE PEOPLE IN AUTHORITATIVE POSITIONS IN YOUR LIFE. TAKE A MOMENT TO BLESS THEM IN PRAYER.

1. _____
2. _____
3. _____

APRIL 2

READ OUT LOUD: 1 Peter 3:14-16 (NIV)

But even if you should suffer for what is right, you are blessed. "Do not fear their threats; do not be frightened." But in your hearts revere Christ as Lord. Always be prepared to give an answer to everyone who asks you to give the reason for the hope that you have. But do this with gentleness and respect, keeping a clear conscience, so that those who speak maliciously against your good behavior in Christ may be ashamed of their slander.

Gentleness is a powerful testimony. It conveys confidence. When you do not fear what others fear, people will want to know why. They will watch you, and many times they will ask where your gentleness comes from. Prepare your answer now.

Gentleness is the royalty of communication. Adorn your speech in its noble clothing.

You are a child of the Most High King.
Talk and act like it.

PRAY A SPECIAL BLESSING OVER A GENTLE PERSON IN YOUR LIFE.

_____
_____
_____
_____
_____

APRIL 3

READ OUT LOUD: Psalm 18:35 (NKJV)

You have also given me the shield of Your salvation; Your right hand supported me, Your gentleness made me great.

When you are tempted to defend yourself, to make it clear to everyone that you are strong, take a moment and stop. Look at what you are doing. You are trying to save yourself, and in trying to save yourself, you are taking the place of Jesus in your life.

Only Jesus can save. You are not your own savior. Jesus is.

One way He will save you from trouble is by showing His gentleness to you and through you.

Be aware of your tone of voice in conversations with others. God will use gentleness to rescue you from every verbal trap that is set for you.

Always remember that gentleness is a potent antidote. It neutralizes the poison of gossip and slander.

APRIL 4

READ OUT LOUD: Proverbs 15:1 (NIV)

A gentle answer turns away wrath, but a harsh word stirs up anger.

Gentleness shuts the mouths of lions with an angelic hand.

ASK GOD TO CLOSE YOUR MOUTH WHEN YOU ARE TEMPTED TO SPEAK SOMETHING HARSH. AND ASK HIM TO USE YOUR GENTLE ANSWERS TO CLOSE THE MOUTHS OF OTHERS.

APRIL 5

READ OUT LOUD: **Philippians 4:5 (NIV)**

Let your gentleness be evident to all. The Lord is near.

Are you known for gentleness?

Is it evident to all?

Is grace your reputation?

Do people approach you in confidence that no matter what they have done, you will give them a gentle response?

Gentleness ushers in the Lord's presence because it declares total dependence upon Him. If you want the people you encounter to encounter Jesus, then let gentleness be the fragrance they inhale when they are around you.

May His presence be what they sense when they are in *your* presence.

May your gentleness show that He is near.

ASK GOD TO MAKE HIS LINGERING PRESENCE OBVIOUS IN YOUR HOME AND OFFICE.

APRIL 6

READ OUT LOUD: James 3:17 (NLT)

But the wisdom from above is first of all pure. It is also peace loving, gentle at all times, and willing to yield to others.

If you are gentle, you will be perceived as wise.

Only a fool or a whale continues to blow hard in order to survive.

Have you ever tried to calm a fussy baby or screaming toddler by being as loud as he is? Did it ever work? No, the way to calm an infant is to get quieter and quieter. The baby will adjust his volume in order to hear you.

You can be the one who is a thermostat for the atmosphere, not negative people. They will meet the temperature that *you* set. Do not rise to the temperature that *they* set.

It is a well-known technique to lower your volume and ease your tone of voice in order to calm an agitated person.

Sure, if you loudly respond, you will see an immediate change, but will it be a *lasting* change?

Model the gentle behavior that you wish others would display.

If you raise your voice, you will likely hear its echo ... in *them*.

APRIL 7

READ OUT LOUD: Galatians 6:1 (NIV)

Brothers and sisters, if someone is caught in a sin, you who live by the Spirit should restore that person gently. But watch yourselves, or you also may be tempted.

Take a moment right now to think back over your own history. Remember a time when you were embarrassed by a teacher's or employer's correction. It probably happened in front of other people, and that is what made it sting.

Gentleness is careful to deliver discipline somewhat privately.

Gentleness protects the heart of the one receiving correction.

USING INITIALS ONLY, ASK GOD TO HELP YOU RESTORE A PERSON WHO NEEDS CORRECTION ... GENTLY.

_____
_____
_____
_____
_____
_____

APRIL 8

READ OUT LOUD: Matthew 11:29 (NIV)

Take my yoke upon you and learn from me, for I am gentle and humble in heart, and you will find rest for your souls.

When Jesus invites you to be like Him, He invites you into a life of rest and peace. That is the way He lived.

He knows you are weary and burdened at times. It is His desire to take the weight off of your shoulders. He presents you with a new yoke: the same one that *He* wears.

A yoke for oxen has two raised spaces, so that the oxen can work side by side. This is the metaphor through which Jesus illustrates His invitation to you. He calls you to take your place on the other side of His yoke. He wants to work side by side with you.

But if you are going to do this, then you must travel at His pace. And His pace will keep your life at peace.

The yoke of Jesus is gentleness and humility.
In order to experience the power of His help, you must walk His way.

APRIL 9

READ OUT LOUD: **2 Corinthians 10:1 (NIV)**

By the humility and gentleness of Christ, I appeal to you—I, Paul, who am "timid" when face to face with you, but "bold" toward you when away!

Be a Christian who lives like a tiger.

A tiger is gentle with its cubs, providing food for them and licking their wounds.

A tiger restrains its power.

Just because a tiger *has* teeth doesn't mean it bares them to its young.

But if anything threatens those cubs, watch out! You will see a tiger's awesome and terrifying strength on display.

Your battle for your loved ones is not against flesh and blood, but against the enemy. Be someone who knows your power, and who understands when to use it.

Learn to restrain your strength when you are with the young or vulnerable and unleash it on their behalf through spiritual warfare.

Be gentle in person.
And ferocious in prayer.

APRIL 10

READ OUT LOUD: **1 Peter 2:23 (NLT)**

He did not retaliate when he was insulted, nor threaten revenge when he suffered. He left his case in the hands of God, who always judges fairly.

You do not have to be your own attorney, defending your decisions to others.

When Jesus was falsely accused, He didn't respond with anything but gentleness, and that was one way He showed His faith. By choosing gentleness, you, too, show your faith.

There is no reason to live like a lawyer when you know the Judge.

OH, RIGHTEOUS JUDGE, I NEED YOU TO STEP IN AND HANDLE _____ FOR ME. HELP ME TO RESIST STEPPING IN FRONT OF YOU AS YOU DO YOUR JOB. HELP ME SURRENDER THE END RESULT.

APRIL 11

READ OUT LOUD: James 1:21 (NLT)

So get rid of all the filth and evil in your lives, and humbly accept the word God has planted in your hearts, for it has the power to save your souls.

A peony is content to grow alone, digging its roots deep and stretching its stalk high without the affirmation of anyone or anything.

A peony develops into tightly wound petals, drooping the head of its heavy bud until the time is right.

And when a peony finally opens to bloom, the blaze of its beauty is unmatched. It doesn't have to scream, it doesn't have to beg, it doesn't have to ask for attention.

The delicate fragrance, the tender color, the grace of its shape are completely irresistible. People are drawn to a peony, and it never has to say a word.

Humbly accept the Word of God planted in you. When it blooms, its gentle power will be overwhelming to everyone around you.

You may never have to say a word.

APRIL 12

READ OUT LOUD: James 2:12-13 (MSG)

Talk and act like a person expecting to be judged by the Rule that sets us free. For if you refuse to act kindly, you can hardly expect to be treated kindly. Kind mercy wins over harsh judgment every time.

You follow a faithful Leader who protects you well. You can trust Him to take care of you.

Exhibit the same type of protective leadership for others. They will eagerly follow you if they know that you are looking out for their true interests. Some of them do not have anyone else who is looking out for them.

Talk about everyone with dignity.
Gently respect and gently protect.

IS THERE SOMEONE IN YOUR LIFE YOU NEED TO DEFEND? PRAY THAT THE LORD WILL GIVE YOU THE RIGHT WORDS AT THE RIGHT TIME.

APRIL 13

READ OUT LOUD: Matthew 5:5 (MSG)

> *You're blessed when you're content with just who you are—no more, no less. That's the moment you find yourselves proud owners of everything that can't be bought.*

These days, people want, want, want.
In a culture of want, contentment is stunning.
Contentment stands out.
Contentment is the bottom line.
It is the thing everyone *really* wants.

Contentment looks and feels like gentleness.
Choose to be content *within* your situation, even if you're not content *with* your situation.

LIST FIVE AREAS IN YOUR LIFE WHERE YOU WILL CHOOSE CONTENTMENT TODAY.

1. _____
2. _____
3. _____
4. _____
5. _____

APRIL 14

READ OUT LOUD: 1 Peter 3:4 (NLT)

You should clothe yourselves instead with the beauty that comes from within, the unfading beauty of a gentle and quiet spirit, which is so precious to God.

A quiet spirit is not necessarily a quiet personality.

You may be gregarious, and you don't need to feel pressured to change. God made you the way you are, and all personality types are necessary to make the earth reflect the jewel tones of heaven.

A quiet spirit is settled assurance.
A quiet spirit is peace and confidence.
A quiet spirit is security.

The opposite of having a quiet spirit is having a spirit that is noisy with need.

DESCRIBE A PERSON YOU KNOW WHO COULD BE SAID TO HAVE A QUIET SPIRIT. WHAT DOES IT LOOK LIKE?

_____
_____
_____
_____
_____
_____

APRIL 15

READ OUT LOUD: Job 15:11 (NIV)

Are God's consolations not enough for you, words spoken gently to you?

When a friend gives a word of encouragement, its effect can last for a few days, even a few weeks.

When God speaks a word of encouragement, its effect can last a lifetime. So make time for Him to speak a gentle word to you today.

Grace is His tone of voice.

DO YOU SEE YOURSELF AS FLAWED OR FAILING? YOU MAY NOT SEE YOURSELF ACCURATELY. ASK GOD TO GIVE YOU THREE DESCRIPTIONS OF HOW *HE* SEES YOU.

1. _____
2. _____
3. _____

APRIL 16

READ OUT LOUD: Ephesians 5:1-2 (MSG)

Watch what God does, and then you do it, like children who learn proper behavior from their parents. Mostly what God does is love you. Keep company with him and learn a life of love. Observe how Christ loved us. His love was not cautious but extravagant. He didn't love in order to get something from us but to give everything of himself to us. Love like that.

Jesus knew there are no well-constructed words that will ever teach more than modeling does.

Have you been trying to impart a lesson to someone in your life? Your instruction is only as good as your example. Choose to be gentle.

Model the positive attitude and behavior you wish to see in another person. That means when your spouse or friends are complaining, take the high road, don't take part. There may be impressionable minds nearby, waiting to see if you are too good to be true.

It is not easy, but it is important to illustrate that people who mean what they say are not unicorns.

They really exist.

APRIL 17

READ OUT LOUD: Psalm 12:5 (MSG)

Into the hovels of the poor, Into the dark streets where the homeless groan, God speaks: "I've had enough; I'm on my way To heal the ache in the heart of the wretched.

Perhaps you have felt God's calling to intentionally serve people who are underprivileged. But don't forget you can set your heart and mind to serve people from *any* walk of life by reacting from a gentle spirit.

You may feel alone as you choose gentleness in an aggressive culture, but that isn't true.

God goes with you.

WRITE A BRIEF DESCRIPTION OF THE GENTLEST THING YOU HAVE SEEN IN NATURE. WHAT PART OF CREATION REPRESENTS GENTLENESS TO YOU?

APRIL 18

READ OUT LOUD: **Deuteronomy 32:2 (NLT)**

Let my teaching fall on you like rain; let my speech settle like dew. Let my words fall like rain on tender grass, like gentle showers on young plants.

When you approach your own Bible reading, it may be a good idea to let yourself take in a little at a time

If you are pressuring yourself to read long passages, there will be days when you don't have time to read that much, so you will skip reading anything at all.

What about reading Scripture in smaller amounts?

Perhaps gentle and consistent nourishment is better for spiritual growth than the pattern of deluge and drought.

LIST FIVE SMALL WAYS YOU CAN NOURISH YOUR SOUL DAILY.

1. _____
2. _____
3. _____
4. _____
5. _____

APRIL **19**

READ OUT LOUD: Philippians 3:19-20 (NIV)

Their destiny is destruction, their god is their stomach, and their glory is in their shame. Their mind is set on earthly things. But our citizenship is in heaven. And we eagerly await a Savior from there, the Lord Jesus Christ.

Sometimes fasting from one meal or fasting for a whole day is a way of pushing the reset button on your priorities.

Are you trying to make a difficult decision at work? You may gain clarity with a fast offered in gentleness and humility.

And the peace of the Lord will be your feast.

WRITE DOWN ONE THING JESUS WOULD LIKE YOU TO FAST FROM FOR A SHORT PERIOD.

_____

_____

HOW LONG WILL YOU FAST FROM IT?

_____

_____

APRIL 20

READ OUT LOUD: **Romans 15:5 (NLT)**

May God, who gives this patience and encouragement, help you live in complete harmony with each other, as is fitting for followers of Christ Jesus. Then all of you can join together with one voice, giving praise and glory to God, the Father of our Lord Jesus Christ.

Unity is a beautiful pursuit.

Diversity can only thrive where there is unity of purpose.

Today is a good day to take a gentle step toward unity by showing someone in leadership your appreciation.

Put your focus on someone in authority in your life today, and think about the extra burden of responsibility that they bear.

LET YOUR LEADERS KNOW THAT YOU SUPPORT THEM BY WRITING A THANK YOU NOTE OR AN EMAIL. THEY WILL READ IT OVER AND OVER AGAIN.

APRIL 21

READ OUT LOUD: **Proverbs 26:1 (NLT)**

Honor is no more associated with fools than snow with summer or rain with harvest.

Some of the restrictions you set for children irritate them. But all of the restrictions you set for them have a purpose. Your expectations are gentle and good.

You want young people to rely on your character and believe that you have their best interests at heart. Children indirectly harm themselves when they test your limits instead of trusting your limits.

The same is true in life. God has set some restrictions for you, and you may feel irritated that He has asked you to wait.

But you can rely on God's character when He doesn't explain His decisions in detail. All of His thoughts toward you have a purpose. They are gentle and good.

You can trust the limits He has set.
It would be foolish to test them.

THANK GOD FOR ONE OF HIS LIMITS IN YOUR LIFE.

APRIL 22

READ OUT LOUD: Proverbs 20:15 (CJB)

A person may have gold and a wealth of pearls, but lips informed by knowledge are a precious jewel.

Keep your eyes on what is most valuable.

Your financial situation may have you wondering if you will ever get to the next level. To you, the next level may be having a little money at the end of the month, it may be freedom from debt, it may be a cushion of savings, it may be the ability to travel or own a lake house.

You probably think the next level will bring you a sense of security.

Before God takes you there, He wants you to realize that your security *will never come from the next level*

The next level is to be enjoyed, not depended upon.

Stop and thank God that *He* is the One Who can be depended upon.

Your knowledge of His greatness is your greatest financial asset.

Be gentle with yourself and stop striving for what's next.

APRIL 23

READ OUT LOUD: 2 Corinthians 6:14-15 (MSG)

Don't become partners with those who reject God. How can you make a partnership out of right and wrong? That's not partnership; that's war. Is light best friends with dark? Does Christ go strolling with the Devil? Do trust and mistrust hold hands?

There are times when prioritizing your faith necessitates taking a step away from situations, places, or people who are working against God and His will for you. There is a way to do that with gentleness.

These people may not be tempting you toward sinful behavior.

They may be tempting you toward doubt.

Be aware that doubt is the most dangerous temptation of all because it appears harmless. But doubt will rob you of the promises God has given you. Doubt is a pickpocket; don't let him stand too close.

With well-chosen words and a warm attitude, kindly tell your friends that you are choosing faith over fear, and that you need them to plant seeds of encouragement, not doubt.

If people continue to war against God's best for you, bow out of those friendships and side with your Faithful Friend.

APRIL 24

READ OUT LOUD: Proverbs 26:17 (NIV)

Like one who grabs a stray dog by the ears is someone who rushes into a quarrel not their own.

A gentle person knows when to get involved.

More importantly, they know when to stay out of it.

Sometimes you can be the most help to a friend when you encourage them to fight their own battles.

Take inventory of your concerns today. Are any of them worries that you are carrying for someone else? Ask the Lord how you can bear another's burdens in the healthiest way.

Perhaps gentleness supports friends and family by encouraging them in what *they* carry rather than by carrying it *for* them.

WRITE DOWN THREE THINGS THAT GOD MAY BE LEADING YOU TO STOP CARRYING FOR ANOTHER PERSON SO THAT THEY CAN CARRY IT FOR THEMSELVES.

1. _____
2. _____
3. _____

APRIL 25

READ OUT LOUD: 1 Corinthians 4:12-13 (NIV)

We work hard with our own hands. When we are cursed, we bless; when we are persecuted, we endure it; when we are slandered, we answer kindly.

How is your heart health? Do you respond in a gentle way *every time*, no matter how you are treated? Do you continue to work for the Lord, even when the people you work for and with do not appreciate you?

A healthy heart responds with love.
It is confident.
It is forgiving.
It is gentle.

A healthy heart responds with love because it is filled with the love of God.

PRAY TO BE FILLED WITH THE LOVE THAT GOD HAS FOR YOU.

APRIL 26

READ OUT LOUD: Ecclesiastes 10:4 (NLT)

If your boss is angry at you, don't quit! A quiet spirit can overcome even great mistakes.

Don't be hasty to make decisions when you are feeling accused. The enemy is an accuser, and he will pierce you with fierce accusations, even when you don't deserve them.

Especially when you don't deserve them.

Take heart. It may not be as bad as you think. And even if it is as bad as you think, it may not end the way you think.

Have you made some waves?
Let God use a gentle spirit within you to quiet them.

ASK GOD TO CALM ANY PROBLEMS YOU MAY HAVE CAUSED AT HOME, AT WORK, OR IN YOUR FRIENDSHIPS.

APRIL 27

READ OUT LOUD: Psalm 107:29 (NIV)

He stilled the storm to a whisper; the waves of the sea were hushed.

Jesus said, "Peace. Be still."

And waves that could have split the boat into pieces were at peace.

It took three gentle words.

What mighty storm do you need to speak to today? It is time to tell it to be still.

IN THE NAME OF JESUS, I SPEAK PEACE TO _____ _____. IT MUST BE STILL. AND IN THE NAME OF JESUS, I ALSO SPEAK PEACE TO MY HEART. IT MUST BE STILL.

APRIL 28

READ OUT LOUD: **Numbers 12:3 (NIV)**

Now Moses was a very humble man, more humble than anyone else on the face of the earth.

Moses was one of the greatest leaders the world has ever known. He moved thousands of people over difficult terrain, and did it faithfully for more than forty years. Many of us would love to have a service record so strong.

You may not think of yourself as the kind of leader who takes people from captivity to freedom.

But God uses you every day to relocate people who are held captive by spiritual bondage.

You humbly and gently lead them to places of freedom.

THINK OF SOMEONE YOU KNOW WHO IS LIMITED OR "TRAPPED." THEN GET CREATIVE. IF THE "PLACE" YOU WANTED TO TAKE THAT PERSON HAD A NAME, WHAT WOULD IT BE? (EXAMPLES: *THE LAND OF PERSONAL RESPONSIBILITY, CONFIDENCE ISLAND, PLANET POLITENESS*, ETC.)

_____

_____

_____

APRIL 29

READ OUT LOUD: **Genesis 33:13-14** (NIV)

But Jacob said to him, "My lord knows that the children are tender and that I must care for the ewes and cows that are nursing their young. If they are driven hard just one day, all the animals will die. So let my lord go on ahead of his servant, while I move along slowly at the pace of the flocks and herds before me and the pace of the children."

When Jacob was traveling with his family across the desert, he understood that the young of his household and the young of his herds needed extra time and a gentle pace to make progress.

You would do well to remember the same thing.
Keep the pace of the children.

ASK GOD IF THERE IS AN AREA WHERE YOU NEED TO SLOW DOWN FOR THE CHILDREN'S SAKE. WRITE DOWN WHAT HE SAYS.

_____
_____
_____
_____
_____
_____

APRIL 30

READ OUT LOUD: Hebrews 5:1-2 (MSG)

Every high priest selected to represent men and women before God and offer sacrifices for their sins should be able to deal gently with their failings, since he knows what it's like from his own experience.

The key to dealing with others gently is dealing with yourself gently.

LIST THREE AREAS OF YOUR LIFE WHERE YOU NEED TO TREAT YOURSELF GENTLER.

1. _____
2. _____
3. _____

MAY

MEDITATIONS ON SELF-CONTROL

[Leaders] must be hospitable, devoted to good, sober-mindedness, uprightness, holiness and self-control.
Titus 1:8 (CJB)

MAY 1

READ OUT LOUD: **Titus 1:8b** (NLT)

[A person] must live wisely and be just. He must live a devout and disciplined life.

It is understandable when you are so worn out that you start subconsciously communicating that you are ready for the weekend, even on Monday morning.

But you are designed to work.

The right amount of work is good.

You may feel frustrated when young people do not have a strong work ethic. So create an environment in your home where a love for work thrives by showing that *you* love working. Even though you may be joyfully anticipating the weekend ahead, remain self-controlled in the way you show it.

Be intentional about your language.

Speak about work as a privilege.

Young people are listening.

They take your words as permission to imitate.

THANK GOD FOR THREE THINGS ABOUT WORK THAT BRING A SMILE TO YOUR FACE (THINK BEYOND THE PAYCHECK).

1. _____
2. _____
3. _____

MAY 2

READ OUT LOUD: 2 Timothy 1:5-6 (NLT)

I remember your genuine faith, for you share the faith that first filled your grandmother Lois and your mother, Eunice. And I know that same faith continues strong in you. This is why I remind you to fan into flames the spiritual gift God gave you when I laid my hands on you.

You work because you are exercising your spiritual gift to make a lasting impact on the world, not because work is your identity.

Your identity is a child of God. And children of God live by faith in their Father.

You cannot control your circumstances, but you can control yourself.

Stoke the fire of your faith. When you do, your spiritual gifts will also grow brighter.

You received your spiritual gifts by faith, and anything you do to increase your faith increases your gifts.

WHAT ARE THE SPIRITUAL GIFTS GOD HAS GIVEN YOU? IF YOU DO NOT KNOW, TAKE TIME TO ASK AND LISTEN TO HIS ANSWER.

1. _____
2. _____
3. _____

MAY 3

READ OUT LOUD: Colossians 3:23 (NLT)

Work willingly at whatever you do, as though you were working for the Lord rather than for people.

Are there fifteen minutes left before the end of your work day? Be self-controlled. Resist the urge to sit at your desk and check social media, giving the vague appearance of work.

There may not be time to start something new, but every moment can be used. Never waste time at the end of the day. Use the last fifteen minutes to pray over your recent projects. Prayer is never a waste of time.

Lean into a change of pace in the final few minutes in the workplace. You don't have to fold your hands and close your eyes. Just open your calendar or planner and put your finger on each approaching deadline or appointment. Ask God to prepare you for those events now and give you favor then.

When someone approaches you and asks what you are working on, it is not awkward or inappropriate for you to say, "I was looking over this month's tasks and praying that God would bless me to do my best." Your colleague may never have seen anyone do that before.

Your prayer can be a quiet witness.

MAY 4

READ OUT LOUD: **1 Corinthians 10:31 (NIV)**

So whether you eat or drink or whatever you do, do it all for the glory of God.

The more stress you feel, the more you may be tempted to let yourself go. But self-control can be for the glory of God.

Love yourself.
Love your body.
You are valuable.

God loves you.
He made your body.
He is the One who determines your value.

You are worth taking care of.
Every single bit of you.

COMMIT TO TAKING CARE OF YOURSELF IN TWO SPECIFIC WAYS THIS WEEK.

1. _____
2. _____

MAY 5

READ OUT LOUD: 2 Timothy 1:7 (NLT)

For God has not given us a spirit of fear and timidity, but of power, love, and self-discipline.

LORD, PLEASE HELP ME TO ELIMINATE FEAR AND TIMIDITY IN THESE AREAS:

___

LORD, SOME AREAS WHERE I NEED POWER, LOVE, AND SELF-DISCIPLINE ARE:

___

MAY 6

READ OUT LOUD: **1 Peter 5:8 (MSG)**

Keep a cool head. Stay alert. The Devil is poised to pounce, and would like nothing better than to catch you napping. Keep your guard up.

Don't sit back and listen to any voice that speaks negatively in your life.

You have survived so many things.

Look at yourself in a mirror and say to yourself, "I am at peace. Nothing can shake the security I have in the Prince of Peace. I can and will be self-controlled no matter what tries to shake me."

The enemy says you will fail.

The Lord says you are an overcomer.

You get to choose who you listen to.

WHAT POSITIVE MESSAGE HAS THE LORD BEEN SPEAKING OVER YOU LATELY?

_____
_____
_____
_____
_____
_____

MAY 7

READ OUT LOUD: 1 Corinthians 9:25 (ESV)

Every athlete exercises self-control in all things. They do it to receive a perishable wreath, but we an imperishable.

A problem is the perfect place for growth.

Help others stay calm in the face of a problem by modeling how *you* stay calm in the face of a problem.

One of the most valuable lessons you will share this year is self-controlled persistence.

There is a reward at the end of a race run well.

ASK GOD TO HELP YOU JUMP OVER YOUR LATEST HURDLE AND FINISH THE RACE WITH SELF-CONTROL.

MAY 8

READ OUT LOUD: Isaiah 65:24 (NIV)

Before they call I will answer; while they are still speaking I will hear.

Jesus listens to the small conversations that happen inside of you. The whispered dialogue between your heart and your head matters to Him.

One moment, you blame yourself for not having self-control. The next, you feel confident and assured in your identity in Christ. Then you wonder again if you ever *will* have self-control. So you take a step back and remind yourself that self-control is Holy Spirit fruit, the result of abiding in the Vine.

Back-and-forth, back-and-forth it goes.

By the time you finally reach out for the answers that come only through prayer, the Lord sends His peaceful reply.

I hear you, dear child, He says.
In fact, I heard you even before you called.

MAY 9

READ OUT LOUD: 1 Corinthians 9:27 (ESV)

But I discipline my body and keep it under control, lest after preaching to others I myself should be disqualified.

It is so easy to think that your soul is the only part of you that matters to God. You have been taught to value the things you cannot see above the things you can see.

You might be forgetting that God loves your body as much as He loves your soul because He made them both.

To have self-control means that your body and soul obey what your God-connected spirit tells them to do.

So tell yourself to get some good sleep.

Take a walk.

Eat well.

He has mighty plans for you on this earth.

His Kingdom is not just about the afterlife.

He wants you to have a healthy soul *and* a healthy body so you can accomplish His purposes *here.*

IS THERE SOMETHING NEW THE LORD IS SAYING HE WANTS TO ACCOMPLISH THROUGH YOU? WRITE ABOUT IT HERE.

_____

_____

_____

_____

_____

MAY 10

READ OUT LOUD: Proverbs 25:28 (ESV)

A man without self-control is like a city broken into and left without walls.

Writing down your core values helps you establish self-control.

When you write down your core values, you create explicit boundaries for yourself. Then you can see the ways that you accidentally trespass on your own desires and dreams.

Put a few walls into place. Rebuild some broken places in your thought life. Force yourself to stay consistent and focused on what truly matters to you.

MY CORE VALUES FOR MY *PERSONAL LIFE* ARE:

_____

_____

_____

_____

MY CORE VALUES FOR MY *PROFESSIONAL LIFE* ARE:

_____

_____

_____

_____

MAY 11

READ OUT LOUD: Proverbs 14:23 (NIV)

All hard work brings a profit, but mere talk leads only to poverty.

Keep plowing.
Keep planting.
God knows how to spread your love thick, even though you may feel you are spread thin these days.
He has a plan for you, and He will see every plan to completion.

Fueled by self-control, persist in your task.
Soon enough you will see the fruit of your labor.

ASK GOD TO TELL YOU THREE TASKS IN WHICH HE WOULD LIKE YOU TO PERSIST.

1. _____
2. _____
3. _____

MAY 12

READ OUT LOUD: 2 Peter 1:5-7 (CJB)

For this very reason, try your hardest to furnish your faith with goodness, goodness with knowledge, knowledge with self-control, self-control with perseverance, perseverance with godliness, godliness with brotherly affection, and brotherly affection with love.

Write a letter to someone who has blessed you

Tell her she was like a gift when you needed her most.

Tell him he believed in you when no one else did.

Tell her you are sorry.

Tell him you are wiser now, and you "get it."

Tell her you took her advice.

Tell him you caught yourself using one of his classic expressions.

Tell her she was right.

Tell him you are doing just fine, and he doesn't have to worry about you anymore.

Tell her she is a big part of who you have become.

MAY 13

READ OUT LOUD: Proverbs 16:32 (NLT)

Better to be patient than powerful; better to have self-control than to conquer a city.

You might think that the most powerful people are those who work *quickly*.

But the most powerful people are those who work *consistently*. Be consistent: to faithfully work and faithfully wait.

Through this you will exhibit the greatest power of all: self-control.

NAME THREE PEOPLE IN YOUR LIFE WHO KNOW HOW TO WORK CONSISTENTLY.

1. _____
2. _____
3. _____

MAY 14

READ OUT LOUD: 1 Peter 4:7 (CJB)

The accomplishing of the goal of all things is close at hand. Therefore, keep alert and self-controlled, so that you can pray.

Prayer changes circumstances.

It accesses power.

A self-controlled person realizes this and stays ready to pray at all times.

Through the *act* of your praying and through the art of your praying, the Lord will bring His heavenly goals to earth.

THANK GOD FOR THREE ANSWERS TO YOUR PAST PRAYERS.

1. _____
2. _____
3. _____

MAY 15

READ OUT LOUD: Titus 2:11-13 (NIV)

For the grace of God has appeared that offers salvation to all people. It teaches us to say "No" to ungodliness and worldly passions, and to live self-controlled, upright and godly lives in this present age, while we wait for the blessed hope—the appearing of the glory of our great God and Savior, Jesus Christ ...

An adult's most vivid memories are often of childhood moments outdoors. In your youth, you used to be fully present when you were outside.

By the time you were an adult, you had learned how to be outdoors in body while indoors in spirit. You may have conditioned yourself to be mentally in the workplace or thinking of things to do when you get home.

Refresh yourself by going outside today.

God's grace will help you be self-controlled and fully present while you are there.

WHERE ARE YOUR FIVE FAVORITE PLACES TO BE OUTSIDE?

1. _____
2. _____
3. _____
4. _____
5. _____

MAY 16

READ OUT LOUD: Romans 12:1-2 (CJB)

I exhort you, therefore, brothers, in view of God's mercies, to offer yourselves as a sacrifice, living and set apart for God. This will please Him; it is the logical "Temple worship" for you. In other words, do not let yourselves be conformed to the standards of the [world]. Instead, keep letting yourselves be transformed by the renewing of your minds; so that you will know what God wants and will agree that what He wants is good, satisfying and able to succeed.

Your body is the temple of God.

You do not have to *go* to a temple as an act of worship. Instead, you get to *give* Him a temple as an act of worship.

DESCRIBE WHAT IT MEANS TO OFFER YOURSELF AS A SACRIFICE IN TODAY'S WORLD.

_____

_____

_____

_____

_____

_____

MAY 17

READ OUT LOUD: Philippians 4:8 (NLT)

Fix your thoughts on what is true, and honorable, and right, and pure, and lovely, and admirable. Think about things that are excellent and worthy of praise.

The word *integrity* comes from the same Latin origin as the word *integer*. An integer is a whole number.

What if a person with integrity is more than just one who tells the truth, but is also one who has the quality of *wholeness*?

The Outside You is comprised of words and actions. The Inside You is comprised of thoughts and feelings. When the Outside You matches the Inside You, there is integrity, or personal wholeness.

If what you think and feel don't match what you say and do, you are just a fraction of what you could be.

ASK THE LORD TO HELP YOU INCREASE IN INTEGRITY.

MAY 18

READ OUT LOUD: James 3:2 (NLT)

Indeed, we all make many mistakes. For if we could control our tongues, we would be perfect and could also control ourselves in every other way.

Pay attention to your speech today. Are there times when you need to apply self-control before you open your mouth?

LOOK UP ONE BIBLE VERSE THAT WILL REMIND YOU OF THE POWER OF YOUR WORDS, AND WRITE IT OUT HERE.

MAY 19

READ OUT LOUD: Psalm 141:3 (NIV)

Set a guard over my mouth, Lord; keep watch over the door of my lips.

Be self-controlled in how to you talk about everyone, even about celebrities and politicians.

You can't expect children to be the kind of people who will try something new and brave in front of others, if they hear you being hypercritical of those in public positions.

It is not enough to tell young people that risks are worth taking.

Let them hear you respecting the ones who have taken them, even if they have made a few mistakes along the way.

THANK GOD FOR THREE PEOPLE YOU ADMIRE FOR TAKING A RISK.

1. _____
2. _____
3. _____

MAY 20

READ OUT LOUD: 2 Thessalonians 3:6-9 (MSG)

Our orders—backed up by the Master, Jesus—are to refuse to have anything to do with those among you who are lazy and refuse to work the way we taught you. Don't permit them to freeload on the rest. We showed you how to pull your weight when we were with you, so get on with it. We didn't sit around on our hands expecting others to take care of us. In fact, we worked our fingers to the bone, up half the night moonlighting so you wouldn't be burdened with taking care of us. And it wasn't because we didn't have a right to your support; we did. We simply wanted to provide an example of diligence, hoping it would prove contagious.

Know when to ask for help from others.
Know when to offer help to others.
Know when to help yourself.

Your self-controlled diligence can be something the Lord uses to instruct others.

ONE AREA YOU NEED TO ASK FOR HELP: _____

ONE AREA YOU NEED TO OFFER HELP: _____

ONE AREA YOU NEED TO HELP YOURSELF: _____

MAY 21

READ OUT LOUD: Proverbs 20:4 (MSG)

A farmer too lazy to plant in the spring has nothing to harvest in the fall.

The way you close a season will have an effect on how you open the next.

You tend to view each spiritual or emotional season as separate and distinct, but they are connected. As you consider how you will make the transition from this one to the next, keep your eyes open.

Lay good groundwork.

Just as it is when you move into a new house, it matters how you transition when you move into a new season. The method with which you pack supplies and furniture will make a difference. You may be tempted to sweep small things into a drawer or dump miscellaneous items into a box today, but will you want to open it later?

A few moments of deliberate preparation now will lead to a big pay-off then.

Sweeping or dumping anything you haven't dealt with creates "baggage" you don't want to carry.

GO BACK TO THAT BOX OR DRAWER IN YOUR HEART AND REORGANIZE IT. ASK GOD TO HELP BECAUSE IT ISN'T SOMETHING YOU CAN DO ON YOUR OWN. YOUR EFFORT WILL BE A GIFT TO YOUR FUTURE SELF.

MAY 22

READ OUT LOUD: Galatians 6:7b-8 (NIV)

A man reaps what he sows. Whoever sows to please their flesh, from the flesh will reap destruction; whoever sows to please the Spirit, from the Spirit will reap eternal life.

Pay attention when the fuel light comes on. Your body is like a reliable car, and if there is a problem, it gives you warnings.

Yet, most people trust a car's warning system more than they trust a human's warning system.

When headaches, arthritis, and stomach pain alert you, you think, "Aww, I can go just a little longer at this pace. I'll slow down soon."

Be self-controlled and make an effort to take care of yourself.

Sow rest today and reap strength tomorrow.

LIST THREE THINGS THAT MAKE YOU FEEL RESTED.

1. _____
2. _____
3. _____

MAY 23

READ OUT LOUD: Proverbs 24:30-34 (NIV)

I went past the field of a sluggard, past the vineyard of someone who has no sense; thorns had come up everywhere, the ground was covered with weeds, and the stone wall was in ruins. I applied my heart to what I observed and learned a lesson from what I saw: A little sleep, a little slumber, a little folding of the hands to rest—and poverty will come on you like a thief and scarcity like an armed man.

Procrastination is a ploy that the enemy uses to make you forget how sweet a harvest tastes.

A heart that is self-controlled works even when it doesn't want to.

If you know what you need to be doing, get busy.

WHAT IS ONE THING YOU KNOW YOU HAVE BEEN PROCRASTINATING? WRITE IT DOWN AND THEN TAKE ONE SMALL STEP TOWARD GETTING IT DONE.

MAY 24

READ OUT LOUD: **Proverbs 27:18 (CJB)**

Whoever tends the fig tree will eat its fruit, and he who is attentive to his master will be honored.

Let young people experience the struggle of an assignment. You don't always have to *directly* answer their questions. God doesn't always *directly* answer yours.

Be self-controlled and help them be attentive to the long work of growth. Try to answer a question with another question. Young people are so proud when they discover something new by themselves.

>   The struggle is crucial.
>   The struggle takes time.
>   The struggle *is* the learning.

THANK GOD FOR YOUR STRUGGLE.

MAY 25

READ OUT LOUD: **Proverbs 27:19 (NIV)**

As water reflects the face, so one's life reflects the heart.

God cares about the condition of your emotional heart. But the condition of your physical heart may be connected to the condition of your emotional heart.

> Let the Holy Spirit give you self-control for both.
> Find healing on the inside first.

IS THERE SOMETHING IN YOUR EMOTIONAL HEART THAT THE LORD WANTS TO HEAL? STOP, PUT YOUR HAND OVER YOUR PHYSICAL HEART, AND PRAY ABOUT IT, INVITING THE LORD TO DO WHAT HE NEEDS TO DO IN ORDER TO BRING TRUTH TO YOUR INNER BEING.

MAY 26

READ OUT LOUD: James 1:19 (NLT)

Understand this, my dear brothers and sisters: You must all be quick to listen, slow to speak, and slow to get angry. Human anger does not produce the righteousness God desires.

Growing up is difficult. A self-controlled and spiritually mature adult deliberately looks for ways to cushion the next generation from the pain that can come through words.

Experienced adults can be so quick with words, and to young people, that can seem like an unfair advantage.

But this is not a time to manhandle anyone. It is the most delicate time of their lives.

Too many other things about growing up can hurt.

USING INITIALS ONLY, PRAY FOR A YOUNG PERSON IN YOUR LIFE WHO IS HURTING AS THEY GROW UP.

MAY 27

READ OUT LOUD: 1 Corinthians 15:33 (NIV)

Do not be misled: "Bad company corrupts good character."

As a child of the King, greatness is in your DNA.

Humility is knowing Who it comes from.

Be self-controlled when selecting close friends. Don't be willing to align yourself with just anybody. Choose friends who know how to reinforce both your greatness *and* your humility.

They can help you keep your balance.

THANK THE LORD FOR THREE FRIENDS WHO HELP YOU KEEP YOUR BALANCE.

1. _____
2. _____
3. _____

MAY 28

READ OUT LOUD: Proverbs 13:3 (NLT)

Those who control their tongue will have a long life; opening your mouth can ruin everything.

If it is not life or death, it probably won't matter in the long run. You do not have to speak up about everything.

And sometimes when you stay quiet, it gives the Holy Spirit a chance to say something.

ASK THE LORD TO HELP YOU STAY QUIET IN AN AREA WHERE YOU FEEL TEMPTED TO SPEAK AT THE WRONG TIME.

MAY 29

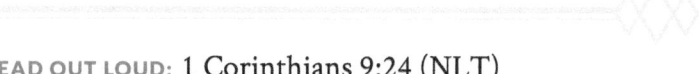

READ OUT LOUD: 1 Corinthians 9:24 (NLT)

Don't you realize that in a race everyone runs, but only one person gets the prize? So run to win!

Submit to the truth that there is a time for every purpose under heaven.

If a contract or a vow is not at stake, you can embrace something new at any time.

Change does not mean failure, especially not a change in favor of your health. Take precious care to avoid unhealthy substances and habits.

Take equal care to avoid unhealthy *circumstances*, such as overwork, busy-ness, stress, lack of community, and lack of rest.

May those around you know that the wisdom you proclaim is also something you are willing to live.

ASK THE LORD IF THERE IS AN AREA WHERE YOU NEED TO START WALKING THE TALK. WRITE DOWN WHAT HE SAYS.

_____
_____
_____
_____
_____
_____

MAY 30

READ OUT LOUD: Ephesians 4:29 (NIV)

Do not let any unwholesome talk come out of your mouths, but only what is helpful for building others up according to their needs, that it may benefit those who listen.

Listening well takes self-control.

Shift your focus from your mouth to your ears.

Listening is about discovering another perspective instead of projecting your own. When you listen in order to understand people, you are better able to build them up according to their needs.

Use your ears to help you *see*.

ASK THE LORD IF THERE IS A PLACE IN YOUR LIFE WHERE YOU NEED TO BE LISTENING MORE THAN SPEAKING. WRITE DOWN WHAT HE TELLS YOU.

MAY 31

READ OUT LOUD: Nehemiah 6:3 (NLT)

I am engaged in a great work, so I can't come. Why should I stop working to come and meet with you?

Nehemiah led a powerful group of people to rebuild the wall around Jerusalem.

Rebuilding the ruined wall was not as difficult as resisting the people who were trying to stop him from working.

Be aware that sometimes, the Lord will ask you to rebuild broken places. This is such an important work that you can expect the enemy will send you distractions and discouragers.

Your answer can be the same as Nehemiah's.

Because you are engaged in a great work, you can't stop now.

WRITE ABOUT SOMETHING THAT HAS BEEN NAGGING AT YOU TO STOP WHAT YOU ARE DOING. ASK GOD TO HELP YOU FINISH THIS GOOD WORK.

_____
_____
_____
_____
_____
_____

JUNE

MEDITATIONS ON TRUST

Trust in the Lord with all your heart, do not depend on your own understanding.

Proverbs 3:5 (NLT)

JUNE 1

READ OUT LOUD: Matthew 11:28-30 (NIV)

Come to me, all you who are weary and burdened, and I will give you rest. Take my yoke upon you and learn from me, for I am gentle and humble in heart, and you will find rest for your souls. For my yoke is easy and my burden is light.

Rest says, "I trust God's work, not my own."

Rest says, "I know God can take care of me better than I can take care of myself."

Rest says, "God can raise up leaders for every position, I do not have to fill them all."

Rest says, "I know that God causes my work to prosper, and He multiplies my efforts."

Rest says, "I can't do it without Him."

NAME A FEW THINGS THAT YOUR OWN REST CAN SAY ABOUT GOD.

1. _____
2. _____
3. _____

JUNE 2

READ OUT LOUD: Mark 6:31 (CJB)

There were so many people coming and going that they couldn't even take time to eat, so he said to them, "Come with me by yourselves to a place where we can be alone, and you can get some rest."

Summer is not a time to quit, but it is a time to change your pace. Trust God with the rhythm of your days.

A healthy pace insists upon time for real rest.

It insists upon time for recreation.

It insists upon time for creation.

It may even include creation without social media *documentation*.

Do you remember doing something for the simple joy of doing it ... without the pressure of sharing a perfect public photograph afterward?

Give yourself permission to go your own way this month, to pursue things just for *joy*.

Don't feel the need to *share* everything.

Live as if Jesus were the only One watching.

JUNE 3

READ OUT LOUD: Jeremiah 31:25 (MSG)

I'll refresh tired bodies; I'll restore tired souls.

Surrender your stress and come to Him for rest. Trust is the offer you can't refuse.

THANK GOD FOR INVITING YOU TO TRUST HIM.

JUNE 4

READ OUT LOUD: Exodus 33:14 (NIV)

The Lord replied, "My Presence will go with you, and I will give you rest."

In the Presence of the Lord, there is no striving.

In the Presence of the Lord, there is rest.

It is one thing to wait. It is another thing to wait and believe at the same time.

Belief added to waiting makes a powerful mixture of trust that accomplishes much.

WRITE ABOUT A TIME WHEN YOU TRULY FELT GOD'S PRESENCE.

_____
_____
_____
_____
_____
_____

JUNE 5

READ OUT LOUD: **Psalm 127:2 (CJB)**

In vain do you get up early and put off going to bed, working hard to earn a living; for he provides for his beloved, even when they sleep.

Rest requires balance.

You can easily spend your time doing nothing. But realize that your "wasted" time is productive when it brings a harvest of laughter or friendship or renewed energy.

Even sleep can be productive, especially when you are laying your head on the tender pillow of trust in God.

Things can happen for you even while you sleep because He never sleeps.

ASK GOD TO HELP YOU SLEEP.

JUNE 6

READ OUT LOUD: Isaiah 30:15b (NIV)

In repentance and rest is your salvation, in quietness and trust is your strength, but you would have none of it.

Rest can save you *from* unnecessary work.
Trust strengthens you *for* necessary work.

THANK GOD FOR FIVE WAYS TO REST THAT HE HAS GIVEN YOU.

1. _____
2. _____
3. _____
4. _____
5. _____

JUNE 7

READ OUT LOUD: 1 John 4:18b (NLT)

If we are afraid, it is for fear of punishment, and this shows that we have not fully experienced his perfect love.

You may think this problem or that trouble is because you have done something wrong.

Don't worry about it, just ask. The Holy Spirit will show you if there is something you need to change.

After you have examined your heart, banish fear by trusting the Lord to show you His incredible care for you.

He loves you, and you don't have to be afraid of *anything*.

TURN OVER A SPECIFIC FEAR THAT HAS BEEN BOTHERING YOU.

_____

_____

_____

_____

_____

_____

JUNE 8

READ OUT LOUD: Isaiah 26:4 (NIV)

Trust in the Lord forever, for the Lord, the Lord himself, is the Rock eternal.

God can be trusted. No person who has ever lived is as trustworthy as He is.

He will never let you down.

His name is Faithful and True, and He will accomplish everything that He has promised you.

He is the Everlasting Rock.

You only *feel* like you are in a free fall.
In reality, your feet are firmly planted.

THANK GOD FOR FIVE BLESSINGS THAT MAKE YOU FEEL SECURE.

1. _____
2. _____
3. _____
4. _____
5. _____

JUNE 9

READ OUT LOUD: Psalm 37:5 (NKJV)

Commit your way to the Lord, Trust also in Him, And He shall bring it to pass.

Sometimes the thing you need to do next is *nothing*.

ASK GOD IF HE WANTS YOU TO DO SOMETHING OR TRUST HIM TO DO IT FOR YOU.

JUNE 10

READ OUT LOUD: Matthew 8:24 (NIV)

Suddenly a furious storm came up on the lake, so that the waves swept over the boat. But Jesus was sleeping.

Trust looks like rest.

No matter what came into Jesus' life, He displayed a heart that was filled with peace. Even when the great storm threatened the safety of his disciples in the boat, He stayed asleep. His disciples thought this meant He didn't care.

Of course He cared.

And what He really wanted for His disciples in that moment was for them to experience the deep rest that comes from trust.

Do you trust God's loving care enough to sleep in your storm?

LIST THREE STORMS GOD HAS CALMED IN YOUR LIFE OVER THE YEARS.

1. _____
2. _____
3. _____

JUNE 11

READ OUT LOUD: Psalm 31:14-15 (NIV)

But I trust in you, Lord; I say, "You are my God." My times are in your hands; deliver me from the hands of my enemies, from those who pursue me.

When you choose trust, you are putting yourself into God's hands.

One of the most tempting things to take back from Him is timing.

You think sooner is better than later, but that may not be so.

When it comes to timing, let go.

IMAGINE YOURSELF LETTING GO OF SOMETHING THAT MATTERS TO YOU. IMAGINE GOD HOLDING IT CLOSE TO HIS HEART WHEN YOU GIVE IT TO HIM.

JUNE 12

READ OUT LOUD: John 14:27 (NLT)

I am leaving you with a gift—peace of mind and heart. And the peace I give is a gift the world cannot give. So don't be troubled or afraid.

Peace is a gift from God and it comes to you in exchange for your total trust in Him.

Everyone else in your life is responsible for accessing their own peace from Him. So don't be surprised when others do not share your peace.

They will question it.

They will doubt it.

They will try to shake it loose from you.

Whether other people acknowledge or validate your peace is irrelevant.

You know what God has given you.

When it comes to promises, hold on.

IMAGINE GOD LETTING GO OF SOMETHING THAT MATTERS TO HIM. IMAGINE YOURSELF HOLDING IT CLOSE TO YOUR HEART WHEN HE GIVES IT TO YOU.

JUNE 13

READ OUT LOUD: Psalm 55:22 (NLT)

Give your burdens to the Lord, and he will take care of you. He will not permit the godly to slip and fall.

It is difficult to watch someone take a risk.

With that in mind, realize that sometimes the people you love might say some discouraging things to you when you embark on new endeavors.

It is not that they think you can't handle it or might fail. It could be that they are protective of your heart.

Forgive the people who discourage you from taking a risk. Though their words may hurt, look for the love that is buried beneath what they say. Thank your friends and family for their loving concern for you, and let them know that you are moving forward with your risk in faith and trust anyway.

Tell them that they don't have to carry the burden of your risk because you have already given that to God.

JUNE 14

READ OUT LOUD: Romans 4:20-21 (NLT)

Abraham never wavered in believing God's promise In fact, his faith grew stronger, and in this he brought glory to God. He was fully convinced that God is able to do whatever He promises.

Pray for someone who is stepping out in faith and trust with their own risk.

You love your child, your friend, or your spouse, and you want to encourage them, but you also have an urge to protect them from getting their hopes up.

Be fully convinced that God can be trusted, no matter the final outcome. Some of the best lessons are learned by losing. Help your loved one stay focused through the ups *and* the downs. Their faith is being trained and is growing stronger throughout the ride.

Their trust brings glory to Jesus.

JUNE 15

READ OUT LOUD: Psalm 112:7 (NLT)

[Those who fear the Lord] do not fear bad news; they confidently trust the Lord to care for them.

The world tells you that you should prepare for heartbreak.

But the children of God don't have to live in a state of *just in case*. You can abandon yourself to the loving care of your Father. Forget your fear of bad news.

Stop pumping the brakes.
Scoot over and let God drive.

LIST THREE AREAS WHERE GOD MAY BE ASKING YOU TO SCOOT OVER AND LET HIM DRIVE.

1. _____
2. _____
3. _____

JUNE 16

READ OUT LOUD: John 4:35 (NLT)

You know the saying, 'Four months between planting and harvest.' But I say, wake up and look around.

The fields are already ripe for harvest.

It won't take as long as you think to accomplish what God has put on your heart.

Perhaps you are worried because you think your promise will arrive in an embryonic state. You feel impatient as you factor in additional time it will need to grow and develop.

But you can trust Him to deliver what you need, when you need it, and *as you need it*. God knows how to accelerate time.

He is capable of giving you a promise that is full grown. Adam entered Eden as a man, not as a baby.

JUNE 17

READ OUT LOUD: Isaiah 50:4 (NIV)

The Sovereign LORD has given me a well-instructed tongue, to know the word that sustains the weary. He wakens me morning by morning, wakens my ear to listen like one being instructed.

God has infused your words with influence.

Trust the power He has put in your tongue.

You co-create with him, and your words build the frame of mind in which you live. Your words establish your atmosphere.

God wakes you up every morning with a supernatural ability to encourage yourself when you are weary, to speak life-giving words over your situation. If you are still and quiet, if you will *listen*, God will teach you exactly what needs to be said to sustain yourself.

You don't have to merely survive.

God will help you use words to create an environment in which you will thrive.

JUNE 18

READ OUT LOUD: Psalm 8:6 (NLT)

You gave [humans] charge of everything you made, putting all things under their authority ...

Both positive and negative emotions are valuable.

No, negative emotions are not wrong, but they can go wrong when you let them rule the day. Emotions should be powerful, but not overpowering.

You have the ability, through the conscious use of your words, to take authority over your emotions.

Tell the darkness to be quiet.
Tell the light to speak up.

SURRENDER YOUR EMOTIONS TO GOD.

JUNE 19

READ OUT LOUD: Psalm 89:8 (NLT)

You are entirely faithful.

God can be trusted.
He won't be *anything* but faithful to you.

ASK GOD TO SHOW YOU IN MEMORABLE WAYS THAT HE IS UTTERLY FAITHFUL.

JUNE 20

READ OUT LOUD: Luke 16:10 (CJB)

Someone who is trustworthy in a small matter is also trustworthy in large ones...

Jesus would never expect you to do something that He has not already done.

He asks you to be faithful with little things as well as big things.

Through this, He is saying that *He* has been faithful with the little things in your life.

He will be faithful with the big things, too.

LIST FIVE LITTLE WAYS GOD HAS BEEN FAITHFUL TO YOU

1. _____
2. _____
3. _____
4. _____
5. _____

JUNE 21

READ OUT LOUD: Psalm 103:2 (NLT)

Let all that I am praise the Lord; may I never forget the good things he does for me.

When it is hard to trust God, remember His goodness to you.

Make some time to reflect on His track record in your life.

Refresh your memory.

WRITE ABOUT A BIG WAY THAT GOD HAS BEEN FAITHFUL TO YOU.

_____

_____

_____

_____

_____

_____

JUNE 22

READ OUT LOUD: Psalm 9:10 (MSG)

God's a safe-house for the battered, a sanctuary during bad times. The moment you arrive, you relax; you're never sorry you knocked.

Run to the Lord when you do not know what to do.

He is the place that always welcomes you. His door swings wide, and He invites you in with a warm embrace. Once inside, He directs you to a seat of honor.

Come in and talk to Him.

No question is small; no request is insignificant.

Even if no one else is paying attention to you, He will.

He can be trusted with your deepest concerns.

When someone you love speaks, you listen to every whisper. How much more will the One who made you lean into the conversation when you speak?

He is eagerly awaiting your visit.

JUNE 23

READ OUT LOUD: Mark 9:24 (CJB)

Instantly the father of the child exclaimed, "I do trust — help my lack of trust!"

Bring Jesus what you have and if you need more, ask Him for it.

The same One who took a small boy's lunch and multiplied it to feed thousands of people can take your simple offering of trust and make it much bigger than it was.

He can give you a level of trust that is greater than you can imagine right now.

But you have to bring Him what you *do* have before He can make it into more.

ASK GOD TO MULTIPLY YOUR TRUST.

JUNE 24

READ OUT LOUD: Psalm 37:25 (NLT)

Once I was young, and now I am old. Yet I have never seen the godly abandoned or their children begging for bread.

God is motivated by the glory of His Kingdom and His name. All of His actions are designed to reveal who He really is.

It would never make sense for Him not to provide for you. It is up to Him to maintain His own reputation as a good Father. You do not have to prove Him. He delights to prove Himself.

Let your prayers move from, "Father, please provide for me," to "Father, thank You in advance for providing for me."

Assumptions about the beauty of His character are good ones to make.

JUNE 25

READ OUT LOUD: **Romans 8:32** (NIV)

He who did not spare his own Son, but gave him up for us all—how will he not also, along with him, graciously give us all things?

How would you live if you had a Father who would spare nothing to show how much He loves you?
What would you ask for?
How would you feel when you pondered your past?
How would you plan for your future?
How would you perceive your present?
Would anything be different?
Could you believe it?

Would you *trust* it?

PRAISE GOD FOR SPARING NOTHING TO SHOW HOW MUCH HE LOVES YOU. IF YOU DO NOT BELIEVE OR FEEL THAT RIGHT NOW, PRAY AND ASK HIM TO HELP YOU UNDERSTAND THAT LEVEL OF LOVE.

JUNE 26

READ OUT LOUD: Psalm 22:4-5 (NIV)

In you our ancestors put their trust; they trusted and you delivered them. To you they cried out and were saved; in you they trusted and were not put to shame.

It will greatly help you to trust God if you get together with another believer and ask them to share stories of times when they trusted God.

The stories they tell you *now* will be like logs you can add to the fire *later*, when your own outlook gets cold and bleak.

Make it a habit to collect testimonies. Ask this question every chance you get: "Tell me about a time when God proved His power and love to you." You will be amazed at the variety of answers you will hear.

They will set your heart ablaze with trust.

LIST THREE PEOPLE YOU CAN ASK TO SHARE THEIR STORY OVER COFFEE OR A MEAL.

1. _____
2. _____
3. _____

JUNE 27

READ OUT LOUD: Romans 4:19-21 (NLT)

And Abraham's faith did not weaken, even though, at about 100 years of age, he figured his body was as good as dead—and so was Sarah's womb. Abraham never wavered in believing God's promise. In fact, his faith grew stronger, and in this he brought glory to God. He was fully convinced that God is able to do whatever he promises.

You might be tempted to think that people who are trusting God are not being realistic. You may think optimism is for the ignorant or naïve.

But trusting God does not mean ignoring your circumstances.

It means looking at your circumstances through God's eyes, instead of your own.

WHEN THE LORD LOOKS AT YOUR MOST CHALLENGING CIRCUMSTANCE, WHAT DOES HE SEE?

___

___

___

___

___

___

JUNE 28

READ OUT LOUD: 1 Samuel 15:17 (NLT)

And Samuel told [Saul], "Although you may think little of yourself, are you not the leader of the tribes of Israel? The Lord has anointed you king of Israel.

Insecurity is the opposite of humility, although they often look similar. Insecurity is actually pride.

When God tells you that He has chosen you, and when He gives you a specific call, purpose, and task, then who are you to say that you are not up to it?

Do you know more than God?

Can you see more than He sees?

Would you dare tell Him, "Yes, but there are things about me that You do not know."

Oh, He knows *everything* about you.
And He chose you anyway.

JUNE 29

READ OUT LOUD: Psalm 21:4-7 (NLT)

[The king] asked you to preserve his life, and you granted his request. The days of his life stretch on forever. Your victory brings him great honor, and you have clothed him with splendor and majesty. You have endowed him with eternal blessings and given him the joy of your presence. For the king trusts in the Lord. The unfailing love of the Most High will keep him from stumbling.

The Lord can give you honor through His triumphs if, *and only if*, you trust Him.

He will not fight a war that you do not turn over to Him.

But if you bring Him your battle, He will give you His victory.

BRING GOD A SPECIFIC BATTLE TODAY.

JUNE 30

READ OUT LOUD: Psalm 33:13-15 (NLT)

The Lord looks down from heaven and sees the whole human race. From His throne he observes all who live on the earth. He made their hearts, so he understands everything they do.

Sometimes it is easier to trust the Lord with the battles you face than it is to trust Him with your feelings.

The One who made hearts knows how they work. He understands your heart and the feelings inside it more than anyone else ever could.

He is not above feelings. In fact, He has His own.

Emotions were *His* idea. He wanted His children to be like Him, and He experiences the full range of emotions, from anger to compassion, from joy to grief.

Trust God with the final frontier: what you *feel*.

LIST FIVE STRONG FEELINGS YOU HAVE BEEN FEELING LATELY.

1. _____
2. _____
3. _____
4. _____
5. _____

JULY

MEDITATIONS ON RENEWAL

Therefore, if anyone is in Christ, the new creation has come: The old has gone, the new is here!
2 Corinthians 5:17 (NIV)

JULY 1

READ OUT LOUD: Psalm 23:1-2 (NLT)

The Lord is my shepherd; I have all that I need. He lets me rest in green meadows; he leads me beside peaceful streams.

Think about how angry the Pharisees were when Jesus healed people on the Sabbath—the day of rest. He timed that on purpose to show them that He works best when His people rest.

May He heal you in your rest.
May He bring true renewal.

May He lead you again and again to quiet waters, to green pastures, and make you *lie down*.

THANK GOD FOR FIVE BLESSINGS OF RENEWAL HE HAS GIVEN YOU.

1. _____
2. _____
3. _____
4. _____
5. _____

JULY 2

READ OUT LOUD: Luke 14:28 (NLT)

But don't begin until you count the cost. For who would begin construction of a building without first calculating the cost to see if there is enough money to finish it?

There is a predictable process to any renewal.

Phase One is Beginning.

Whether it is losing weight, making a quilt, writing a book, beginning a graduate program, or renovating the kitchen, you may feel overwhelmed to begin.

But thinking and planning are necessary steps, and you have taken them.

Be encouraged. You may be well past Phase One of your renewal.

You have *already* begun.

JULY 3

READ OUT LOUD: 2 Corinthians 8:11 (NIV)

Now finish the work, so that your eager willingness to do it may be matched by your completion of it, according to your means.

The challenge in *Phase Two* of the renewal process is maintaining momentum in the *Working*.

Your home may be filled with the fossils of abandoned projects. You knitted most of the scarf but never finished the edge. You straightened half of the closet, but never completed the other half. You painted most of the baseboards, but never got to the area behind the couch.

Allow yourself no more than a two-day break from working during Phase Two.

Momentum is everything.

JULY 4

READ OUT LOUD: Ecclesiastes 9:10 (NIV)

Whatever your hand finds to do, do it with all your might, for in the realm of the dead, where you are going, there is neither working nor planning nor knowledge nor wisdom.

People don't talk much about the stage called *Improvising*, which is *Phase Three* in the renewal process. You look around at accomplished people and imagine that they always know exactly what they are doing. As a result, when a confusing snag interrupts your own process, you assume that the whole project is irreparable.

When you reach a point of confusion, you can quit or you can improvise.

Improvisation may be a key ingredient to achievement. Ask a few successful (and honest) friends, and they may confess that there were times that they had no idea what to do next, but they kept going, anyway.

As it turns out, "winging it" can be another way to fly.

JULY 5

READ OUT LOUD: Jeremiah 1:10b (MSG)

Your job is to pull up and tear down, take apart and demolish, And then start over, building and planting.

By the time you get to *Phase Four* of the renewal process, you may want to ignore it. Phase Four is *Revising*.

Almost everything needs revising. Think of it as "revisiting." Go back to the beginning and revisit how you would do things differently if you had known *then* what you know *now*.

Do not risk skipping Phase Four, though it will be tempting to do so.

Revising is the difference between mediocrity and excellence.

JULY 6

READ OUT LOUD: Ecclesiastes 7:8a (NLT)

Finishing is better than starting.

Phase Five in the renewal process is *Finishing*.

There comes a time to be done.

Don't lose weight without getting rid of the old clothes and buying new ones. Don't make a quilt without binding the edge. Don't write a book without publishing it. Don't start a graduate degree without completing the dissertation. Don't renovate the kitchen without bringing every drawer, cabinet, and faucet back to working order.

Phase Five is when you need a kick in the pants. Sometimes you will receive it from others, but most of the time, you have to offer it to yourself.

Tape a note to your bathroom mirror today.
On it, write: *You can't say you did it until it's done.*

JULY 7

READ OUT LOUD: Isaiah 43:18-19 (NIV)

Forget the former things; do not dwell on the past. See, I am doing a new thing! Now it springs up; do you not perceive it? I am making a way in the wilderness and streams in the wasteland.

The Author of Life never stops rewriting life stories. Every day, God's "To-Do" is to renew.

HOW HAS GOD REWRITTEN YOUR LIFE STORY?

JULY 8

READ OUT LOUD: John 10:4 (NLT)

After he has gathered his own flock, he walks ahead of them, and they follow him because they know his voice.

God is ahead of you. He started your renewal program years ago.

Your Good Shepherd will level the path for your feet.

And because He goes ahead of you, you are not behind.

THANK GOD THAT HE GOES AHEAD OF YOU. ACKNOWLEDGE THE AREAS WHERE IT IS CLEAR THAT HE HAS.

_____

_____

_____

_____

_____

_____

JULY 9

READ OUT LOUD: John 13:34-35 (MSG)

Let me give you a new command: Love one another. In the same way I loved you, you love one another. This is how everyone will recognize that you are my disciples—when they see the love you have for each other.

As you make an effort to renew your heart, there are three basic questions that should guide you.

Here is the first: How are your *people*?

Are you plugged in? Involved? Listening? Being heard? Has it been too long since you went out and had fun? Are you taking good care of the ones who need it? Are you taking good care of yourself? Is everyone safe?

ANSWER THOSE QUESTIONS HERE:

JULY **10**

READ OUT LOUD: Matthew 6:24 (NIV)

No one can serve two masters. Either you will hate the one and love the other, or you will be devoted to the one and despise the other. You cannot serve both God and money.

As you make an effort to renew your heart, there are three basic questions that should guide you.

Here is the second: How are your *values?*

You may say you value the Bible. Are you reading it? You may say you value writing, relaxing, playing, socializing, exercising. Are you doing it? You may say you value integrity. Are you living it? You may say you value freedom from debt and distraction. Are you choosing it? Is the stuff that matters accounted for?

ANSWER THOSE QUESTIONS HERE:

_____

_____

_____

_____

_____

_____

_____

_____

_____

JULY 11

READ OUT LOUD: Psalm 37:23 (NLT)

The Lord directs the steps of the godly. He delights in every detail of their lives.

As you make an effort to renew your heart, there are three basic questions that should guide you.

Here is the third: How is your *direction*?

Are you headed the right way? Are you following God? If you are, then you will end up exactly where you need to be.

ANSWER THOSE QUESTIONS HERE:

JULY 12

READ OUT LOUD: John 15:1 (NLT)

I am the true grapevine, and my Father is the gardener.

Whether you are planning to make a list of concrete goals this year or if you are trying to do something vague, like changing your mindset, recognize that you are not alone in your desire to grow.

God wants you to grow more than you want yourself to grow.

Would you expect anything less from the Master Gardener?

ASK GOD FOR FIVE WAYS HE WANTS YOU TO GROW.

1. _____
2. _____
3. _____
4. _____
5. _____

JULY 13

READ OUT LOUD: John 6:63 (NLT)

The Spirit alone gives eternal life. Human effort accomplishes nothing. And the very words I have spoken to you are spirit and life.

God is not neutral when it comes to renewal.

It is His favorite subject.

You do not have to compartmentalize, only consulting Him when you are in trouble or when you need help in your spiritual life.

You are a spiritual being in an earthly body. Anything that involves you is part of your spiritual life. So ask the Holy Spirit for help in all things, not just "spiritual" things.

Make prayer your first priority every day.

WHAT ARE TWO THINGS THAT YOU CAN SAVE UNTIL LATER IN THE MORNING SO THAT YOU CAN PUT PRAYER FIRST?

1. _____
2. _____

JULY 14

READ OUT LOUD: Galatians 6:9 (NIV)

Do not become weary in doing good, for at the proper time, we will reap a harvest, if we do not give up.

Hearts will stay hungry if you walk away from the harvest now.

ASK GOD TO HELP YOU KEEP GOING IN THE SPECIFIC AREA WHERE YOU FEEL LIKE QUITTING.

JULY 15

READ OUT LOUD: **Habakkuk 3:17-19 (NIV)**

Though the fig tree does not bud and there are no grapes on the vines, though the olive crop fails and the fields produce no food, though there are no sheep in the pen and no cattle in the stalls, yet I will rejoice in the Lord, I will be joyful in God my Savior. The Sovereign Lord is my strength; he makes my feet like the feet of a deer, he enables me to tread on the heights.

Maybe you need to ask yourself if God is enough.

INSPIRED BY THE MODEL OF THE POETIC VERSE ABOVE, WRITE OUT YOUR "THOUGH" STATEMENTS.

THOUGH _____

THOUGH _____

THOUGH _____

THOUGH _____

YET I WILL REJOICE IN THE LORD.

JULY 16

READ OUT LOUD: Ecclesiastes 7:8 (CJB)

The end of something is better than its beginning, so the patient are better than the proud.

Have you considered that impatience is a form of pride? *Humbly* ask the Lord to help you wait for your renewal.

USE THIS SPACE TO EXPRESS YOUR SUBMISSION TO GOD'S TIMING.

_____

_____

_____

_____

_____

_____

JULY 17

READ OUT LOUD: Habakkuk 2:2 (CJB)

Write down the vision clearly on tablets, so that even a runner can read it.

Add an imaginative dimension to renewing yourself today.

Think about what you want your life to look like this time next year.

Sharpening your vision helps you see how to get there.

WHAT WILL YOUR LIFE LOOK LIKE IN TEN YEARS? IN TWENTY? IN THIRTY?

_____

_____

_____

_____

_____

_____

JULY 18

READ OUT LOUD: 2 Corinthians 1:20 (NIV)

For no matter how many promises God has made, they are "Yes" in Christ. And so through him the "Amen" is spoken by us to the glory of God.

When God makes a promise to you, Jesus says, "Yes!" and you say, "Amen!"

Don't expect Him to give you something you don't believe He will give you.

WHAT HAS JESUS SAID YES TO IN YOUR LIFE? WHAT DO YOU SAY AMEN TO?

AMEN TO: _____

AMEN TO: _____

AMEN TO: _____

AMEN TO: _____

AMEN TO: _____

JULY **19**

READ OUT LOUD: **Revelation 21:4 (ESV)**

He will wipe away every tear from their eyes, and death shall be no more, neither shall there be mourning, nor crying, nor pain anymore, for the former things have passed away.

Just because you have been in a negative circumstance or frame of mind in the past does not mean that you will stay that way forever.

There is freedom for you. Ask God how to unlock the door that has trapped you. Sometimes you allow the enemy to walk into your life through emotions such as bitterness, jealousy, anger, and unforgiveness.

When Satan walks into your life, he always locks the door behind him.

But Jesus has the keys.

TELL THE LORD ABOUT A DOOR YOU NEED HIM TO UNLOCK.

JULY 20

READ OUT LOUD: Ephesians 4:21 (ERV)

I know that you heard about him, and in him you were taught the truth. Yes, the truth is in Jesus.

Tell yourself the Truth every day. You cannot change what you do not see accurately. Sometimes you make yourself feel better by telling yourself that your bad habits are not so detrimental. But that little self-deception may not be helpful.

Jesus came to bring lasting change. He is able to do that because He is Truth and only Truth all the time. He sheds light where there has been shadow and illuminates your understanding.

Let Jesus acquaint you with the Truth about yourself so that He has space to renew your spirit and mind.

JULY 21

READ OUT LOUD: Psalm 51:10 (NLT)

Create in me a clean heart, O God. Renew a loyal spirit within me.

It doesn't matter where you have been and what you have done, God has the power to make you new.

To believe otherwise is to say that your shortcomings are more powerful than God's ability to re-create.

LIST THREE PLACES YOU DESIRE GOD'S RENEWAL.

1. _____
2. _____
3. _____

JULY 22

READ OUT LOUD: **Romans 10:9 (NIV)**

If you declare with your mouth, "Jesus is Lord," and believe in your heart that God raised him from the dead, you will be saved.

Your *eternal life* in heaven depends on Christ alone. The only effort you make is to declare His sovereignty with your mouth and believe His authority with your heart.

He does all the rest. It is that simple.

In the same way, your *abundant life* on earth depends on Christ alone. The only effort you make is to align your actions and beliefs with His Word.

He does all the rest.
It is that simple.

WHAT DO YOU THINK IS GOD'S DEFINITION OF ABUNDANT LIFE HERE ON EARTH?

_____

_____

_____

_____

_____

_____

JULY 23

READ OUT LOUD: Deuteronomy 30:14 (NIV)

No, the word is very near you; it is in your mouth and in your heart so you may obey it.

God has pre-wired you to love His Word. If it seems like a chore to spend time reading the Bible, then ask Him to help you see all of the benefits it offers.

Treasures are waiting for you.
Dive in and find them.

ASK GOD TO HELP YOU FALL IN LOVE WITH HIS WORD.

JULY 24

READ OUT LOUD: 1 Corinthians 6:20 (NIV)

> ... *you were bought at a price. Therefore honor God with your bodies.*

The loudest lesson you teach is one you never speak.
It is the lesson other people see in you.

Is your hope in God *visible*?

THANK GOD FOR FIVE PEOPLE WHO EXHIBIT VISIBLE HOPE.

1. _____
2. _____
3. _____
4. _____
5. _____

JULY 25

READ OUT LOUD: Matthew 4:4 (NIV)

Man shall not live on bread alone, but on every word that comes from the mouth of God.

Contrast the hunger of the body to the hunger of the heart.

You are not surprised when your body feels hungry again and again. You feed it multiple times a day.

Then why are you surprised when your heart feels hungry again and again? Why do you think you should be able to nourish it once a day and be done?

The next time you feel heart pangs throughout the day, apply a generous helping of grace to the ache, and ask yourself what you are *really* hungry for.

It is probably Jesus.

JULY 26

READ OUT LOUD: Romans 15:4 (NIV)

For everything that was written in the past was written to teach us, so that through the endurance taught in the Scriptures and the encouragement they provide we might have hope.

Heartache means you are hungry for heaven and Him again.

Spiritual nourishment doesn't always last until evening, any more than breakfast cereal does.

Plant heaven into your plot of earth, grow a garden, and feed your heart some *real* food.

Reach for spiritual nourishment often.

BY YOUR OWN SELF-ASSESSMENT, HOW OFTEN WOULD YOU SAY YOU REACH FOR SPIRITUAL NOURISHMENT THROUGHOUT THE DAY?

JULY 27

READ OUT LOUD: Matthew 5:6 (MSG)

You're blessed when you've worked up a good appetite for God. He's food and drink in the best meal you'll ever eat.

Jesus is the Bread of Life. Until He comes for you, you can expect to be hungry here.

But there is good news: Those who hunger and thirst for Him *will be filled.*

ASK JESUS TO INCREASE YOUR HUNGER FOR HIM.

JULY 28

READ OUT LOUD: Psalm 72:6-7 (NLT)

May the king's rule be refreshing like spring rain on freshly cut grass, like the showers that water the earth. May all the godly flourish during his reign. May there be abundant prosperity until the moon is no more.

Pray that your words will be refreshing and renewing, both to you and to the people who hear them.

May your communication cause light to break through many clouds.

May it cause joy to breakthrough the dullest of days.

DESCRIBE A TIME WHEN YOU SAW LIGHT DAWN IN SOMEONE'S LIFE BECAUSE OF SOMETHING YOU DID OR SAID.

___

___

___

___

___

___

JULY 29

READ OUT LOUD: Psalm 45:1 (NIV)

My heart is stirred by a noble theme as I recite my verses for the king; my tongue is the pen of a skillful writer.

Let your heart be stirred by a noble theme. Does one of these words grab you?
Enjoy.
Begin.
Bless.
Wait.
Open.
Build.
Rise.
Courage.
Slow.
Relax.

Look for ways you can meditate on these simple pleasures and turn them into praise.

Reach for the themes that stir your heart.

WAS THERE A NOBLE THEME (FROM THE LIST ABOVE OR OTHERWISE) THAT STIRRED YOUR HEART TODAY? WHAT WAS IT?

_____

JULY 30

READ OUT LOUD: Acts 3:20 (NLT)

Times of refreshment will come from the presence of the Lord ...

You look forward to spending time with delightful friends and family.

That is how God feels about spending time with *you*.

SET ASIDE TWO TO FOUR HOURS FOR DEEP SPIRITUAL RENEWAL BEFORE THE SUMMER IS OVER. MAKE A PLAN TO GET AWAY BY YOURSELF WITH A JOURNAL AND YOUR BIBLE AND ASK THE LORD TO SPEAK TO YOU ABOUT WHATEVER IS ON HIS MIND.

JULY **31**

READ OUT LOUD: Psalm 41:1-2 (NLT)

Oh, the joys of those who are kind to the poor! The Lord rescues them when they are in trouble. The Lord protects them and keeps them alive. He gives them prosperity in the land and rescues them from their enemies.

The beauty of God's economy is that there is always a return. No sooner do you empty your storehouse than Jesus fills you up again.

Refresh another person, and He will respond.

God wants to give more to you today.
You can give Him a reason.

AUGUST

MEDITATIONS ON PREPARATION

Commit to the Lord whatever you do, and he will establish your plans.

Proverbs 16:3 (NIV)

AUGUST 1

READ OUT LOUD: 1 John 4:16 (NIV)

And so we know and rely on the love God has for us. God is love. Whoever lives in love lives in God, and God in them.

Are there days you wonder whether God is paying attention to your prayers? That is a love question. You are not really questioning whether He listens to you but whether He *loves* you.

A person who feels loved, feels heard.

If you are not feeling heard, please ask God to remind you that He loves you. Prepare for whatever's next by settling this in your heart before you do anything else. Just ask Him to communicate His love.

Then pay attention and listen.

Remember, God wants to feel heard, too.

RECORD THE WAYS THAT GOD SHOWS AND TELLS YOU THAT HE LOVES YOU.

_____

_____

_____

_____

_____

AUGUST 2

READ OUT LOUD: Romans 8:28 (NLT)

And we know that God causes everything to work together for the good of those who love God and are called according to his purpose for them.

Try something new. Try to expect blessing every morning. When God says that He will work all things for your good, He means it. He has a plan, just like you do. His purpose overrides anything that you could think of. You base decisions upon interacting with an *ideal* family member or friend, one who doesn't exist. Real people are imperfect, but God knows them, inside and out. He created them. He made their minds, He honed their hearts, and He will direct you to do what is best for yourself *and* for them. He loves all of His children, and He gave a calling to each one.

You are not the only person in the room He has called. Jesus is going to work for the good of *all* of you.

IF YOU SUMMARIZED YOUR CALLING IN ONE SENTENCE, WHAT WOULD IT BE?

_____

_____

_____

_____

AUGUST 3

READ OUT LOUD: Psalm 40:17 (MSG)

Let those who know what you're all about tell the world you're great and not quitting. And me? I'm a mess. I'm nothing and have nothing: make something of me. You can do it; you've got what it takes—but God, don't put it off.

Stop right now and put a sticky note on this page. Label it: *When I want to give up.*

As the year progresses and the stresses increase, you might want to give up. That is when you need to turn back to this page.

Here is a trustworthy rule: When you find yourself at a dead end, go back to *where* you started and remember *why* you did.

USE THIS SPACE TO RECORD WHAT YOU WOULD SAY TO SOMEONE WHO WAS READY TO GIVE UP. WRITE A FEW WORDS TO REMIND YOURSELF WHY YOU DO WHAT YOU DO. YOUR FUTURE SELF WILL BE GLAD YOU DID.

_____

_____

_____

_____

_____

AUGUST 4

READ OUT LOUD: Ephesians 3:20-21 (NIV)

Now to him who is able to do immeasurably more than all we ask or imagine, according to his power that is at work within us, to him be glory in the church and in Christ Jesus throughout all generations, for ever and ever! Amen.

God is at work within you.
His presence is with you to comfort and protect.
To inspire and direct.
To lead you toward blessings you don't expect.

As you go through your day, remember that He is able to make the impossible, possible.

You pray for blessing and help. And once you pray for something, you expect it. But now He is inviting you to move past the daily things you expect and onward toward the unexpected—a territory of pure imagination. Ask yourself: In what ways can you go further with God and imagine more?

He is able to exceed your expectation.
Better yet, He is able to exceed your *imagination*.

AUGUST 5

READ OUT LOUD: **Ephesians 1:5 (NLT)**

God decided in advance to adopt us into his own family by bringing us to himself through Jesus Christ. This is what he wanted to do, and it gave him great pleasure.

God's purpose for you began long before you were born. He knew what He was doing when He created you. He chose you and brought you into His family. You are intentionally designed, and you are wanted.

You are *not* a mistake.

Not a single thing about you is a mistake.

He is a good Father. Fathering is His favorite thing to do. He would never leave you to figure it out alone. The moment you ask for help, God is there. He kneels beside you, like a daddy joining His child in a project. He enjoys getting into the details of your life. Spending time with you warms His Father-heart. He loves showing you how to do things and guiding you toward what's next.

IN THE MIDDLE OF AN ORDINARY TASK TODAY, CLOSE YOUR EYES FOR A MOMENT AND PICTURE YOUR HEAVENLY FATHER BESIDE YOU.

AUGUST 6

READ OUT LOUD: 2 Corinthians 4:7-9 (NIV)

But we have this treasure in jars of clay to show that this all-surpassing power is from God and not from us. We are hard pressed on every side, but not crushed; perplexed, but not in despair; persecuted, but not abandoned; struck down, but not destroyed.

Sometimes you feel inadequate, or at the very least, you feel *ordinary*.

Good news: God loves using ordinary things.

The faithful Potter wants to hold His glory and goodness in vessels that He made by hand. The next time you are overwhelmed by your own "ordinariness," thank God that your ordinariness is the very thing that makes you a perfect container for His power.

He made you and He will use ordinary you to accomplish extraordinary things this year. He loves to show that His mighty power is always at work.

THANK HIM FOR THREE WAYS HE HAS SHOWN HIS POWER THROUGH YOUR ORDINARY LIFE.

1. _____
2. _____
3. _____

AUGUST 7

READ OUT LOUD: **Proverbs 21:5 (MSG)**

Careful planning puts you ahead in the long run; hurry and scurry puts you further behind.

Often, the planning stages of something important can take longer than the event itself.

Find pleasure in the process. The more you prepare, the more successful you will be. Planning creates margin for those times when a guest drops by or something goes wrong.

The temptation will be to procrastinate. You might think you want to rest now and prepare later.

Preparation will not rob you of rest, it will only move the resting forward to a moment when it will be sweeter... *after* the work is done. If you rest *before* the work is done, it is not real rest. You'll feel better if you don't procrastinate.

Don't let the work keep working on your mind.
Get it done.

ASK GOD FOR HIS HELP TO COMPLETE TWO IMPORTANT THINGS IN A TIMELY WAY.

1. _____
2. _____

AUGUST 8

READ OUT LOUD: **Proverbs 16:3 (NIV)**

Commit to the Lord whatever you do, and he will establish your plans.

Exceptional leaders have curious minds. As you lead others, seek to experience life as if it were brand new to you. Think about science as a discoverer. Approach math inquisitively. Engage literature with the heart of a brand new reader. Look at history as if you don't know what happens next. Enter the arts as a doorway to your soul.

The God of science can see everything from the atom to the outer reaches of the universe at the same time. The God of mathematics understands dimensions that we do not yet know. The God of literature knows how every story fits into His Story. The God of history has been present for every moment of it. And the God of the arts? Well, the One who created every kind of flower knows a little bit about creativity.

The King of kings and Lord of lords is also the Leader of leaders. When you don't know what to do next...

Simply raise your hand and ask.

AUGUST 9

READ OUT LOUD: Proverbs 16:9 (NLT)

We can make our plans, but the Lord determines our steps.

Think of planning as a kind of investment. It can save you headache and heartache. Instead of making bold assumptions about how much you will be able to accomplish, sit down in humility, holding your professional calendar and your personal calendar side-by-side. Look at the busiest times of the year and reconsider *everything*. Remember, you are a holistic being. Your personal life and professional life have to work well together.

Have you ever abandoned a project because you happened to schedule it too close to the flurry of Thanksgiving and Christmas? Have you lost interest at work because you decided to tackle a highly-detailed task the week before a difficult emotional anniversary? Have some of your best efforts been derailed by your own distraction because a friend got married, you sold your house, or a family member had an important graduation?

These personal events matter. Plan accordingly. Take an afternoon to measure the days ahead, looking with fresh eyes.

God can reveal a pothole you may have overlooked. He'll help you steer around it.

AUGUST 10

READ OUT LOUD: Proverbs 19:21 (NIV)

Many are the plans in a person's heart, but it is the Lord's purpose that prevails.

You and the Lord can dream *together*.

Set a timer for fifteen minutes, then pray, asking God to give you His ideas for the coming season. Is there something He wants to do that you haven't thought of?

Let the wild ideas have a little room on the dance floor. You never know what God will do once they are there.

BE STILL AND LISTEN TO THE LORD. WRITE DOWN EVERYTHING THAT HE BRINGS TO YOUR MIND. DO NOT TRY TO EDIT THE LIST AS YOU GO. DO NOT TRY TO FILTER OUT IDEAS THAT YOU THINK ARE YOUR VOICE FROM IDEAS THAT MAY BE HIS VOICE.

1. _____
2. _____
3. _____
4. _____
5. _____
6. _____
7. _____

AUGUST 11

READ OUT LOUD: James 4:13-15 (NIV)

Now listen, you who say, "Today or tomorrow we will go to this or that city, spend a year there, carry on business and make money." Why, you do not even know what will happen tomorrow. What is your life? You are a mist that appears for a little while and then vanishes. Instead, you ought to say, "If it is the Lord's will, we will live and do this or that."

Effective preparation is done in humility. Pride prepares but then doesn't accept interruptions to the plan. Pride is rigid, not ready.

There is a difference.

When you prepare in humility, you leave some space for the Holy Spirit to work. He may change the direction of your journey right in the middle of it. This is not pulling a trick on you. He is keeping you in a constant relationship with Him. You will be most effective if you depend upon Him to work in you as well as in those around you. Even if a task is underway, do not feel hesitant to shift it if He leads you to.

God knows how your words and efforts are landing.

He might be the One who is prompting you to alter your approach to the runway.

AUGUST 12

READ OUT LOUD: Isaiah 32:8 (NLT)

But generous people plan to do what is generous, and they stand firm in their generosity.

You may not know every circumstance waiting on the horizon, but you know *yourself.*

Choose now how you will behave, no matter what happens. What will your primary response be?

Do you want to be known as *generous?*
Decide to respond as a generous person would.
Do you want to be known as *merciful?*
Decide to respond as a merciful person would.
Do you want to be known as *hopeful?*
Decide to respond as a hopeful person would.

Stand firm in the attribute you have chosen to develop this year.

HOW DO YOU WANT TO BE KNOWN?

WRITE YOUR WORD HERE:_____

AUGUST 13

READ OUT LOUD: Proverbs 24:3-4 (NLT)

A house is built by wisdom and becomes strong through good sense. Through knowledge its rooms are filled with all sorts of precious riches and valuables.

Phenomenal life exists where the stewarded skill and Spirit-led wisdom of a believer intersect.

If you use your training and experience to build your storehouse of skill, the Lord will fill that house with His supernatural blessings. He will supply things such as keen insight and overflowing mercy.

Skill is not enough.
Only a relationship with God supplies true riches.

LIST THREE EXAMPLES OF "TRUE RICHES" THAT GOD HAS GIVEN YOU.

1. _____
2. _____
3. _____

AUGUST 14

READ OUT LOUD: Psalm 127:1-2 (NLT)

Unless the Lord builds a house, the work of the builders is wasted. Unless the Lord protects a city, guarding it with sentries will do no good. It is useless for you to work so hard from early morning until late at night, anxiously working for food to eat; for God gives rest to his loved ones.

Go home on time today. You don't have to stay and keep working until after everyone else is gone.

Look ahead, cancel your weekend plans to work, and leave some unallocated hours for yourself and your family and friends. Use those hours to rejuvenate your heart and mind. Trust that God is doing a lot of work on your behalf, and you can afford to relax.

Rest is one of His sweetest gifts to you.
Don't leave the package unopened.

ASK GOD TO EASE YOUR MIND SO THAT YOU CAN REST.

AUGUST 15

READ OUT LOUD: 2 Chronicles 20:22 (NLT)

At the very moment they began to sing and give praise, the Lord caused the armies of Ammon, Moab, and Mount Seir to start fighting among themselves.

In one of those stunning biblical accounts that would make a great movie, King Jehoshaphat looked out upon the landscape and began to shake. Vast armies moved against the Israelites, and he knew he had no chance of victory. He was under-resourced and about to be overwhelmed. The unsure king knelt before God, calling out to his only hope. God told him not to worry. The battle would belong to the Lord, and the Israelites would never have to fight.

The next morning, the men of Israel were battle-ready, but when they walked forward, they didn't draw their swords. Instead, they began to sing. They praised God, and the attacking armies began fighting *themselves*! The enemy never advanced against the people of God.

You will face many skirmishes this year. Chances are, you will be under-resourced and overwhelmed. That is the moment you must praise.

Let worship go before you.
God will win your wars before you get there.

AUGUST 16

READ OUT LOUD: 2 Timothy 2:15 (NIV)

Do your best to present yourself to God as one approved, a worker who does not need to be ashamed and who correctly handles the word of truth.

A parent bears the great responsibility of shaping a first impression of things. Many times, the way a parent interacts with the community of God will either turn off a child forever or lay a foundation upon which to build a life. You hope that your children will leave home and create habits that are inspired by a love of the Lord and His church from their youth.

Look ahead to the moment when you will introduce an aspect of Christianity to them for the first time. Think of it the same way you would think of arranging a blind date for someone you care about.

It is not that different.

You want your children to fall in love with Jesus.

Prepare the perfect introduction, so that it is more likely to happen.

AUGUST 17

READ OUT LOUD: Proverbs 21:31 (NLT)

The horse is prepared for the day of battle, but the victory belongs to the Lord.

It cannot be said enough: God is in charge.

There is nothing you can do well if you do it on your own. Choose to run with God. He will fight for you. But you must prepare, just the same. Express to the Lord that you are in full cooperation with Him. He doesn't want to do it all on His own, either. He *can*, but He probably *won't*.

Doing your *part* helps you both enjoy your *part*nership.

LIST ONE BATTLE THAT YOU WILL PREPARE FOR WITH YOUR WHOLE HEART. REMEMBER, YOU ARE A HOLISTIC PERSON. IT MIGHT BE FROM ANY AREA IN YOUR LIFE.

I COMMIT TO PARTNERING WITH GOD BY PREPARING FOR
THE BATTLE OF _____ IN MY LIFE.
I KNOW THAT EVERY EFFORT WILL BE WORTH IT WHEN HE
WINS THE VICTORY.

AUGUST 18

READ OUT LOUD: Hebrews 11:7a (NIV)

By faith Noah, when warned about things not yet seen, in holy fear built an ark to save his family.

Noah's work still astounds.

He hammered away on a boat for 100 years, and during the building phase, he never saw a drop of the rain he expected. He operated on faith for what was to come.

If God has spoken purpose into your life, but you are waiting to see evidence of what He has promised, then keep working with Noah-strength. It may take longer than you thought, but it *will* come.

And when it does, you will be ready.
Stay fueled by faith.

LIST THREE TASKS FOR WHICH YOU NEED GOD TO GIVE YOU NOAH-STRENGTH TO KEEP GOING.

1. _____
2. _____
3. _____

AUGUST **19**

READ OUT LOUD: James 3:1 (NIV)

Not many of you should become teachers, my fellow believers, because you know that we who teach will be judged more strictly.

Don't get too agitated when people judge you. Assessment and evaluation come naturally to humans.

The truth is, you should feel proud of yourself for stepping onto the stage of scrutiny for a good cause: to bravely carry out God's calling on your life. Not many people are willing to do that. And those who aren't willing also aren't qualified to assess or evaluate you.

The opinions of those who have never walked in your shoes should be listened to with caution. Some tasks are harder than they think.

Beware of any words that aren't clothed in grace.

WRITE A DECLARATION OF INDEPENDENCE, A STATEMENT THAT ASSERTS YOUR COMMITMENT TO WORK FOR GOD'S APPROVAL ALONE.

_____
_____
_____
_____

AUGUST **20**

READ OUT LOUD: Hebrews 11:6 (NIV)

And without faith it is impossible to please God, because anyone who comes to him must believe that he exists and that he rewards those who earnestly seek him.

Why does God receive faith as such a pleasurable offering to Him? Why is it impossible to please Him without it?

Because faith is the place in your life where God is on the throne. If you have faith, then God has somewhere to sit down and rule in your life. If you do not have faith, He cannot take control the way you need Him to. Having faith is like saving a seat for God.

The *pilot* seat.

Without faith, you are still the one in charge.

How do you know if you have faith? One way you can assess your faith-level is by reviewing your life over the last few weeks. Have you obeyed what He has been asking you to do?

Faith is always measured by obedience.

LIST THREE AREAS WHERE YOU ARE MOVING OUT IN BOLD FAITH THIS YEAR.

1. _____
2. _____
3. _____

AUGUST 21

READ OUT LOUD: **Hebrews 6:10 (NIV)**

God is not unjust; he will not forget your work and the love you have shown him as you have helped his people and continue to help them.

No one knows how to reward like God does.

He has vast storehouses of blessing, and He can't wait to pour them out on you. He won't miss one little detail of your life and work. He doesn't take His eyes off you.

Even if people take you for granted, God does not take you for granted. If you are overlooked, forgotten, and unrecognized on earth, you will be noticed, remembered, and honored in spiritual ways.

Wait for it.

TAKE SOME TIME TO NOTICE GOD'S WORK THE SAME WAY HE NOTICES YOURS. THANK HIM FOR THREE BLESSINGS YOU DO NOT WANT TO TAKE FOR GRANTED.

1. _____
2. _____
3. _____

AUGUST 22

READ OUT LOUD: 1 Corinthians 3:12-15 (NIV)

If anyone builds on this foundation using gold, silver, costly stones, wood, hay or straw, their work will be shown for what it is, because the Day will bring it to light. It will be revealed with fire, and the fire will test the quality of each person's work. If what has been built survives, the builder will receive a reward. If it is burned up, the builder will suffer loss but yet will be saved—even though only as one escaping through the flames.

Think of God as your ultimate Evaluator. He is the One who will review how you have lived at the end of your lifetime. He is the One who will assess your work and determine its value.

This should not incite fear as you live your life, but should give you great relief. You are not accountable to an employer who does not care about you. The One who loves you most is the One who will evaluate you.

He made you, and your success is His success.
Work for *Him*.

IN WHAT WAY DOES WORKING FOR GOD LOOK OR FEEL DIFFERENT THAN WORKING FOR HUMANS?

_____

_____

_____

AUGUST 23

READ OUT LOUD: Psalm 19:9-11 (NIV)

The fear of the Lord is pure, enduring forever. The decrees of the Lord are firm, and all of them are righteous. They are more precious than gold, than much pure gold; they are sweeter than honey, than honey from the honeycomb. By them your servant is warned; in keeping them there is great reward.

Some ordinary tasks can feel painful or irritating at times. This is just one more reason to work for the Lord and not for people. His commands, His laws, His decrees, are sweet. They always bring life. Ask Him to help you carry out the aspects of living that are *not* favorable to you. He will give you supernatural power to view them differently. Ideas became laws because someone, somewhere, thought they would be good for people.

THOUGH IT MAY SEEM COUNTER INTUITIVE, ASK GOD TO HELP YOU THINK OF REASONS WHY A TASK THAT YOU DISLIKE COULD BE GOOD FOR YOU.

AUGUST 24

READ OUT LOUD: Ephesians 1:18 (NLT)

I pray that your hearts will be flooded with light so that you can understand the confident hope he has given to those he called—his holy people who are his rich and glorious inheritance.

Ask God to open your eyes.
He will give you vision.

Ask God to open your ears.
He will give you discernment.

Ask God to open your mind.
He will give you wisdom.

Ask God to open your heart.
He will give you empathy.

TODAY, THANK HIM FOR SPECIFIC SKILLS HE HAS GIVEN YOU.

1. _____
2. _____
3. _____
4. _____

AUGUST 25

READ OUT LOUD: **Matthew 6:3-4 (NIV)**

But when you give to the needy, do not let your left hand know what your right hand is doing, so that your giving may be in secret. Then your Father, who sees what is done in secret, will reward you.

No one else will know. They won't know how much money you have spent. They won't know how much time you have spent.

They won't know how much effort you have spent praying, planning, waiting, blessing, writing, emailing, calling, hoping, trying, celebrating. They will not know how much you have invested.

But God knows.

Make peace with the fact that He might be the *only* One who knows how hard you work. He is the One you are living for anyway. Make peace with the fact that few will thank you. The work is worth doing anyway. Make peace with your purpose. It was never about recognition for you.

You don't obey God because you want to *receive* a blessing.

You obey God because you want to *be* one.

AUGUST 26

READ OUT LOUD: 2 Peter 1:3 (NLT)

By his divine power, God has given us everything we need for living a godly life. We have received all of this by coming to know him, the one who called us to himself by means of his marvelous glory and excellence.

You cannot calculate your inner strength. There is no way to sum up the wealth of your experiences. Jesus has used every moment of your life and has prepared you for this day. Every past disappointment, every past recovery, every past failure, every past victory ... all of these have made you ready.

A soldier becomes better with each battle. The same is true for you. Sometimes you worry that your training or education is not what you would like it to be. Don't forget that the entire world is a classroom. You have been absorbing, growing, and changing your whole life long.

You may not possess an official document for your heart qualifications, but you need to be aware of them, just the same. Face each day knowing you are prepared. You have what it takes, and others need what you have.

They need *you*, not your credentials.

AUGUST 27

READ OUT LOUD: 1 Chronicles 17:8 (CJB)

I have been with you wherever you went, I have destroyed all your enemies ahead of you; and I am making your reputation like the reputations of the greatest people on earth.

Share a short story from your life with the next generation today. Make some real connections with young people by deliberately telling some memories this year. But spare your listeners the minute details, unless they ask for more. Respectfully honor their attention spans. You can offer enduring truths without oversharing. Keep it brief.

Charles Dickens wrote more than 358,000 words to tell the story of *David Copperfield*, and less than 29,000 words to tell the story of Scrooge in *A Christmas Carol*. Dickens knew the power of a shorter story.

Sometimes less is more.

LIST THREE MEANINGFUL MEMORIES YOU COULD SHARE.

A FUNNY STORY: _____

A POIGNANT STORY: _____

A SUSPENSEFUL STORY: _____

AUGUST 28

READ OUT LOUD: Ecclesiastes 9:10a (NIV)

Whatever your hand finds to do, do it with all your might.

Remember that other people have thought about this day as much as you have. They have prepared for it in their own way.

In fact, they have thought about this entire year, filling it with their hopes. They have envisioned good times with friends and success at work. They have determined that this will be their best year yet.

Just like you have.

They bring an expectant heart when they walk through the door of your life. Some look like they care, and some look like they don't care. But don't let them fool you. *Everybody* cares how they are treated.

Give your best to *each person*.
Not just to the ones who treat you well first.

AUGUST 29

READ OUT LOUD: Isaiah 30:21 (NIV)

Whether you turn to the right or to the left, your ears will hear a voice behind you, saying, "This is the way; walk in it."

People will come to you with all kinds of wounds this year, some potentially fatal to their Kingdom success. Your home can be an Intensive *Care* Unit, where you invite Jesus to be the Great Physician. Never remove spiritual life support. Never give up or stop caring.

You already know, deep in your heart, that you are prepared to handle trauma. You may not want to face it, but if necessary, you know you can.

For some people, one dedicated Christian can mean the difference between a lifetime of 'paralysis' or truly moving toward all they were meant to be.

ASK GOD TO HELP YOU BRING TRUTH AS AN ANTIDOTE TO THE PARALYZING LIES OTHERS MAY HAVE BELIEVED ABOUT THEMSELVES.

AUGUST 30

READ OUT LOUD: **Matthew 7:24 (NIV)**

Therefore, everyone who hears these words of mine and puts them into practice is like a wise man who built his house on the rock.

It is easy to make promises and hard to keep them.

Think twice, three times—*four!*—before you say something that will inspire expectation in others, especially children. The higher their hopes, the more disappointed they will be if you don't follow through.

The kind of person who deliberately shows consistency will earn respect. This is not to say there is no room for grace. There is room for grace *and* need for it. Grace teaches good lessons. But consistency teaches good lessons, too. Live consistently. Let your words be the foundation of your character. If you say something, do it.

Establish yourself now as someone who can be trusted.

Your life will be better for the bedrock it was built upon.

AUGUST 31

READ OUT LOUD: Ephesians 2:10 (NIV)

For we are God's handiwork, created in Christ Jesus to do good works which God prepared in advance for us to do.

This year is part of the plan.

All of this good work was prepared in advance for you to do.

You are not waiting for your real life to begin. You may alter your role one day. You may move. But today you are here. Don't let your mind wander to any other time or any other place. Set aside moments to dream of the future, but don't shortchange the people who are counting on you to be *present* in the present.

This year is more valuable than you know.

Like one more facet on the surface of a diamond, it will make your life shine brighter.

Every experience adds brilliance.

THANK GOD FOR THREE OF YOUR "FAVORITE YEARS" YOU HAVE LIVED SO FAR.

1. _____
2. _____
3. _____

SEPTEMBER

MEDITATIONS ON LOVE

Love is patient, love is kind. It does not envy, it does not boast, it is not proud. It does not dishonor others, it is not self-seeking, it is not easily angered, it keeps no record of wrongs. Love does not delight in evil but rejoices with the truth. It always protects, always trusts, always hopes, always perseveres. Love never fails.

1 Corinthians 13:4-8 (NIV)

SEPTEMBER 1

READ OUT LOUD: Proverbs 15:13 (MSG)

A cheerful heart brings a smile to your face; a sad heart makes it hard to get through the day.

Some people will tell you that you must be stern in order to get compliance from young people. But no one perceives authority on the basis of a facial expression. Some scowling people receive no respect at all.

Even when a parent has done an excellent job of conveying consistent expectations, there are still times when children misbehave. One of the easiest things a parent can do when that happens is to *stop smiling*. The more peaceful and pleasurable a home is, the less interference it takes to change the atmosphere. Excessive words are not necessary when one disappointed look will do. But you have to smile at lot *first* before you can have a smile to take away.

If your children grow accustomed to your pleasant face every day, they will miss it when it is gone.

And they will adjust their behavior in order to see that smile return.

SEPTEMBER 2

READ OUT LOUD: Matthew 25:40 (NIV)

Truly I tell you, whatever you did for one of the least of these brothers and sisters of mine, you did for me.

People tend to spend time thinking how they could live better if they had *just one more thing* ... that piece of technology, that well-lit workspace, that talented assistant, the removal of that irritating person or situation. You have spent time thinking about these things, too.

The truth is, you already have what it takes to live well. Living a good life requires a big heart. A big heart is the most valuable thing you will ever need. It is your greatest resource, and you already have it. A big heart isn't something you have to wait for. It has nothing to do with experience. Twenty-somethings don't have to worry about not having enough, and eighty-somethings don't have to fear running out.

Lead with love. Love isn't up to anyone but *you*.

Every time you show someone that you care, you're showing Jesus that you care about *Him*.

SEPTEMBER 3

READ OUT LOUD: Matthew 5:16 (MSG)

Here's another way to put it: You're here to be light, bringing out the God-colors in the world. God is not a secret to be kept.

Let go of stress and feel God's love for you. Go outside and enjoy these last bright moments of summer before the days dress in autumn. Bring that brightness with you everywhere.

Someone you will see today feels a perpetual gray cloud in their hearts. You are the sunny day they need so badly. You may have thirty years to interact with that person, and you may have only thirty seconds.

How can you make a difference in thirty seconds?

You can smile.

You can be courteous.

You can listen.

Others will need the love that you absorb for yourself *today*. So soak up the sun and God's goodness while you can.

Whether they express it or not, people long for you to shine into their lives.

SEPTEMBER 4

READ OUT LOUD: Psalm 16:8-9 (NIV)

I keep my eyes always on the Lord. With Him at my right hand, I will not be shaken. Therefore my heart is glad and my tongue rejoices; my body also will rest secure.

There are moments in life when your response will be sudden and involuntary. A situation can surprise you, almost taking the breath right out of your chest. But the majority of the time, you have the opportunity to choose your response in advance. You can make a conscious decision to respond well.

Decide to laugh.

To smile.

To be warm and welcoming.

To do what love would do.

God is love.

Do as He does.

This choice will saturate your life, setting the daily tone for the hundreds—maybe thousands—of people who will walk through the door of your world this year.

Make the decision about *how* you will respond before you *have* to respond.

SEPTEMBER 5

READ OUT LOUD: **Luke 14:10 (NIV)**

But when you are invited, take the lowest place, so that when your host comes, he will say to you, 'Friend, move up to a better place.' Then you will be honored in the presence of all the other guests.

Look over your life with fresh eyes. Is there anyone who is being ignored or forgotten?

That person is now your *Person of Great Value*. Subconsciously, you will turn your gaze toward your *Person of Great Value*. You will pay attention to her. You will invite her to share her opinion. You will give the person in the *overlooked situation* the best of you. And no one in between will be lost in the shuffle.

Your favor will flow naturally, because you have planted the seed in your mind. It may seem like an insignificant change to make because it is only a change in your thought life. But you don't always need to roll out a big, new, shiny program in order to produce results. Sometimes a mental shift will do it. The motivation behind this shift is love.

> Love invites us to take a better seat.
> Love always looks and feels like an upgrade.

SEPTEMBER 6

READ OUT LOUD: 2 Corinthians 5:18-19 (NIV)

All this is from God, who reconciled us to himself through Christ and gave us the ministry of reconciliation: that God was reconciling the world to himself in Christ, not counting people's sins against them. And he has committed to us the message of reconciliation.

As a Christian, you are a reconciler. Reconciling is settling the differences. It is making two versions of the same account agree.

Think of it this way. If your list of financial transactions and the bank's list of financial transactions do not match, they must be reconciled. If there is a mistake to be found, it is most likely somewhere in your calculations.

Reconcile people to God's truth. Reconcile people to His love. If they have seen themselves as having very little value, the mistake can be found somewhere in *their* calculations. Because in God's record of the account, they are priceless.

And so are you.

ASK GOD TO TELL YOU THREE VALUABLE THINGS HE SEES IN YOU.

1. _____
2. _____
3. _____

SEPTEMBER 7

READ OUT LOUD: Isaiah 43:1b (NIV)

Do not fear, for I have redeemed you; I have summoned you by name, and you are mine.

Try to speak others' names as often as possible.

Why say, "What do you think?" or "Thanks for that insight!" When you can say, "Mary, what do you think?" or "Thanks for that insight, Chris!"

It may feel awkward at first, but something happens when people hear their own name. A statement or question without a name attached is like a gift-wrapped present without a bow. It is not a big deal when it is missing, but it is so much nicer when it's there.

Say a name often to show you care.

THANK GOD FOR FIVE PEOPLE WHO CARED FOR *YOU* WELL WHILE YOU WERE GROWING UP.

1. _____
2. _____
3. _____
4. _____
5. _____

SEPTEMBER 8

READ OUT LOUD: Malachi 2:10 (NLT)

Are we not all children of the same Father? Are we not all created by the same God?

People enjoy hearing the names of the ones they love. Make an effort to say someone's name when you talk to their parents, siblings, or close friends. This may seem obvious, but if you pay attention, you will notice that after you say a person's name once, you tend to use pronouns for the rest of the conversation. Parents especially love to hear their children's names. Keep in mind that the name a parent chose for their child is sweet and tender to their ears. Say that name, and you will have their full attention.

God is a loving parent, too.

He enjoys hearing the names of His children. Pray for others by name, even if you just read down a list.

Pray a blanket of blessing over people, as you say their names.

You will have their Heavenly Father's full attention.

MAKE TIME TODAY TO PRAY OVER A LIST OF PEOPLE FROM YOUR WORK OR CHURCH OR FAMILY BY NAME.

SEPTEMBER 9

READ OUT LOUD: James 1:19 (NIV)

My dear brothers and sisters, take note of this: Everyone should be quick to listen, slow to speak and slow to become angry.

That person who has not been saying much has a lot going on in his or her heart.

Quiet people may not speak because they are not sure you want to hear what they have to say. Maybe someone in their past told them that their opinion didn't matter. Maybe they aren't sure that you won't do the same thing. They *want* to believe you, but they aren't sure they can.

What if you intentionally asked for their input? They may say they "don't care" at *first*, and over time, they will come to realize that you really are interested.

Can you delegate a meaningful responsibility to them? Start with that small act of sharing, and you may find that it encourages more participation in the days to come.

Prepare a place of unconditional love to help quiet people communicate. Never force it. Give them time to develop trust. Be patient.

And when they finally share, stop everything and give them your full attention and honor.

Accept their early and tentative efforts.

SEPTEMBER **10**

READ OUT LOUD: Ephesians 3:17b-19 (NIV)

I pray that you, being rooted and established in love, may have power, together with all the Lord's holy people, to grasp how wide and long and high and deep is the love of Christ, and to know this love that surpasses knowledge—that you may be filled to the measure of all the fullness of God.

God has planted you in the rich soil of His love, and your roots receive the nutrients of His constant care.

The strength that people can see in you comes from a deep, deep place that they cannot see.

The love that flows into you when you commune with Christ will later flow out of you in the form of spiritual fruit that will nourish others.

The Fruit of the Spirit is love ...

Love is something given to you by His Spirit.
Love is something you give to others by your spirit.

SEPTEMBER 11

READ OUT LOUD: 2 Timothy 3:16-17 (NIV)

All Scripture is God-breathed and is useful for teaching, rebuking, correcting, and training in righteousness, so that the servant of God may be thoroughly equipped for every good work.

God can never be taken out of schools and workplaces because He lives in you, and you are there. The more you faithfully read and live from the Word of God, the more it will equip you to do His work anywhere you go.

Remember that when it comes to your job, you are not there to make disciples; you are there to make differences.

You are the disciple in the room. Let others see that being a disciple of Jesus *means* making a difference.

Who else can bless like one who knows where blessings come from? At work, you do not have to evangelize in a way that is awkward. Why tell the message of the cross when you can live it out? Why display a Bible when you can live like someone who knows what it says. When they see your example, people will ask you questions about what makes you different, and then you can answer with the gospel.

The more you love like a child of God, the more others will be drawn to your Father.

Loving well is how you sing the song of Jesus, even when you can't speak His name.

SEPTEMBER 12

READ OUT LOUD: Lamentations 3:22-23 (NLT)

The faithful love of the Lord never ends! His mercies never cease. Great is his faithfulness; his mercies begin afresh each morning.

Most people don't expect perfection from you because they don't want *you* to expect it from *them*. Perfectionism sets an impossible standard for everyone. If you don't love *yourself* just as you are, how are others going to believe you love *them* just as they are?

You may be hard on yourself when things are not exactly as you hoped they would be this year. Your routines may not solidify. You may fall behind on your plans. Your kitchen, your laundry, your desk may be a mess. Don't worry.

Your family won't remember that *you* had a clean house every evening.

They will remember that *they* had a clean slate every morning.

LIST THREE AREAS WHERE YOU WILL START LOVING YOURSELF JUST AS YOU ARE:

1. _____
2. _____
3. _____

SEPTEMBER 13

READ OUT LOUD: Luke 6:36 (NIV)

Be merciful, just as your Father is merciful.

Remember that the *picture* of mercy is a *pitcher* of mercy.

Whatever fills a pitcher pours out. Reject perfectionism and accept God's mercy instead. You will pour out on others whatever has filled you.

Sometimes people could benefit from love and discipline, and sometimes they could benefit from love and mercy. Pray that God will show you which one they need.

Living in the balance of discipline and mercy is what it means to love.

ASK GOD TO GIVE YOU WISDOM FOR A SPECIFIC ISSUE YOU HAVE BEEN EXPERIENCING WITH A CHALLENGING PERSON.

SEPTEMBER 14

READ OUT LOUD: Romans 12:6-7 (NIV)

We have different gifts, according to the grace given to each of us. If your gift is ... teaching, then teach.

Some people have a go-to gift for baby or wedding showers. They don't use the gift registry and head straight for the package of diapers or a certain set of kitchen utensils they always like to give. This makes it easy to pass along a present. There is not a long ceremonious effort to try to select a gift. Also, because they always know what they will bring, they never have to arrive empty-handed.

God gave you a go-to *spiritual gift*, as well. It prepares you for countless days ahead. You always know what you can bring to the party, and through His loving provision, you never have to arrive empty-handed.

YES, YOU HAVE GIFTS. ASK GOD TO REVEAL TO YOU OTHER GO-TO GIFTS HE'S GIVEN YOU. WRITE DOWN WHAT HE SAYS.

SEPTEMBER 15

READ OUT LOUD: Luke 6:40 (NIV)

The student is not above the teacher, but everyone who is fully trained will be like their teacher.

You teach people a lot just by being who you are. Let your community see your character.

- Tell the truth.
- Give generously.
- Show compassion.
- Respect authority.
- Speak well of others.

Your character is important because people learn more from actions than from words. They learn more from love than from lessons.

Whether you realize it, you will influence the development of *their* character. Be faithful even when it is hard. Be friendly and likable, too.

If they *like* you, they will want to be *like* you.

Show them a heart that the world wouldn't mind seeing in duplicate.

SEPTEMBER 16

READ OUT LOUD: 1 Corinthians 13:3 (MSG)

If I give everything I own to the poor and even go to the stake to be burned as a martyr, but I don't love, I've gotten nowhere. So, no matter what I say, what I believe, and what I do, I'm bankrupt without love.

Love is the only way anyone learns.
    Love is the only way anyone learns.
    Love is the only way anyone learns.

ASK GOD TO HELP YOU LOVE LIKE HE DOES.

SEPTEMBER 17

READ OUT LOUD: Hebrews 10:39 (NIV)

But we do not belong to those who shrink back and are destroyed, but to those who have faith and are saved.

Courtesy is a dying art. The next time you see a person younger than twenty, model the appropriate way to greet someone. Offer warm words of welcome. Extend a handshake, giving an example of how to interact with self-assurance.

Even teenagers have trouble with decent handshakes. They are about to enter a world where an assertive handshake says so much. It conveys that they are ready, eager, and will not shrink back. They need this basic skill as much as they need verbal skills. Look them in the eye. Show them how to stop staring at the floor or a device, to lift their chins and look up. Model how they should engage another person from a place of confidence.

Face-to-face.
Heart-to-heart.
Right from the door.
Right from the start.

SEPTEMBER 18

READ OUT LOUD: Deuteronomy 32:2 (NLT)

Let my teaching fall on you like rain; let my speech settle like dew. Let my words fall like rain on tender grass, like gentle showers on young plants.

Discover the power of encouraging words. Your words may be the only nourishment that some people ever hear.

The next time you speak life-giving words of encouragement to someone, notice how their face changes. Watch the way their features soften. A furrowed brow relaxes. A narrowed eye opens. A tight mouth breaks into a smile. This is not unlike dry soil that softens under the gentle flow of water.

The wilting plant stands up again.

Is someone you know walking with bent shoulders? Is his or her head hanging low?

Place them under the gentle flow of your love and watch them rise.

THANK GOD FOR THREE PEOPLE WHO ENCOURAGED YOU WHEN YOU FELT LIKE YOU WERE WILTING.

1. _____
2. _____
3. _____

SEPTEMBER **19**

READ OUT LOUD: Proverbs 18:1 (NKJV)

A man who isolates himself seeks his own desire; He rages against all wise judgment.

One of the ways we strengthen ourselves for life and work is by connecting with other believers.

Much is being said and written about introverts these days. Maybe you recharge within the quiet of home. It may be that you agree with the idea that small talk is a big weight to bear.

At times, you may prefer to avoid a large group, like at church. It is easier than ever to stay home and "attend church" online. These days, people can cocoon their whole family away from others by choosing forms of church that don't involve getting to know the messy people there. It is possible to be isolated, even if you go and just sit on the back row, never having a real conversation with anyone.

Do you see the danger ahead?

The enemy prowls like a predator, looking for the unprotected family or individual. They are an easy target. God has provided love as a barrier against assault. Love binds people together. Love surrounds the camp like a force field.

Stay involved with the church—the community of love.

God gave us each other for a reason.

SEPTEMBER 20

READ OUT LOUD: Proverbs 18:9 (NIV)

One who is slack in his work is brother to one who destroys.

You're on in ten ... nine ... eight ... seven ...

Wait.

You thought you could take a break today? Just coast? Slack off? Relieve your racing mind by going on autopilot at work?

Yes, but your brain and heart are so interconnected. It is hard to turn off one without turning off the other. That is why those days when you are on autopilot never have as much life, love, or energy. They are dull, dutiful, and flat. When you turn off your mind, you turn off your heart, too.

Sure, everyone has those "autopilot" days.

But too many of those will have a high price tag: the loss of that magic that makes you so special.

SEPTEMBER 21

READ OUT LOUD: Matthew 10:31 (NIV)

So don't be afraid, you are worth more than many sparrows.

Young people are curious about what you were like when you were *their* age. Pick something to tell them.

- What was your favorite recess game?
- Describe your first car. Who taught you to drive?
- Describe your first job. Did you quit or were you fired?
- Tell about a time you worked hard for something.
- Tell about a time you didn't get something you wanted.
- Tell about a time you made a sacrifice and gave a gift that was hard to give.

Remember that young people resent stories that do not have a point. Don't waste their time. But don't miss an opportunity to connect with them in a genuine way, either. Love always moves toward connection.

Your life has great worth. Offering one of your age appropriate stories every once in a while is like extending a hand to the next generation. It is hard for them to picture you as a young person. Help them realize that you have been where they are.

This is one more way of saying, "We are not that different, after all."

SEPTEMBER 22

READ OUT LOUD: Matthew 7:12a (NIV)

So in everything, do to others what you would have them do to you.

Some of the people who are desperate for love will beg for it, fight for it, and wrestle it away from every other person in the room. When they do this, they create a scenario that is the opposite of what they need. They irritate you and make it almost impossible for you to give them the warmth of your positive attention. Naturally, you try to change them by ignoring them.

You do this because you think the negative attention will make a difference. You use pressure to create peace. But it won't work that way.

These needy people feel your negative attention like a chill in the room, and it only makes them want more warmth. So they try harder to receive it, and the cycle continues. They do not understand how to attain what they desire (though it may seem obvious to you), and they are envious of people who *do* know how to get your positive attention.

Just give them the warmth they long for, even when you feel like turning a cold shoulder. Treat them as you would treat people who communicate well. Then expect a difference over time.

Someone who is warm eventually stops begging for a coat.

SEPTEMBER 23

READ OUT LOUD: Psalm 56:8 (MSG)

You've kept track of my every toss and turn through the sleepless nights, Each tear entered in your ledger, each ache written in your book.

There is an option on a multiple choice test that test-makers know as *the distractor*. It looks right and seems right. But it is not the *most* right. Test-takers are tempted to choose this answer if they are not paying close attention.

The same thing can happen to you. You are not taking a multiple choice test, but there will be a distractor for you, just the same.

Heartache can be a distractor. Instead of focusing on your hurts, let God be the One to keep track of them. Giving your pain to Him in prayer throughout the day takes it off of your shoulders.

Teach people how to take good care of others by taking good care of *them*.

Teach them how to take good care of themselves by taking good care of *yourself*.

SEPTEMBER 24

READ OUT LOUD: 1 John 4:7-8 (MSG)

My beloved friends, let us continue to love each other since love comes from God. Everyone who loves is born of God and experiences a relationship with God. The person who refuses to love doesn't know the first thing about God, because God is love—so you can't know him if you don't love.

God is love.

The way to know God is to love someone.

And the way to know God better than you have ever known Him before is to love someone who is hard to love.

USING ONLY THE INITIALS OF THEIR NAME, WRITE A PRAYER, ASKING GOD TO HELP YOU LOVE SOMEONE WHO IS HARD TO LOVE.

_____
_____
_____
_____
_____
_____
_____

SEPTEMBER 25

READ OUT LOUD: Ephesians 4:16 (NIV)

From him the whole body, joined and held together by every supporting ligament, grows and builds itself up in love, as each part does its work.

There is synergy in together-work.

Why try to operate with your own diminishing reserves of energy, when you have access to the miracle of synergy? The impossible is made possible when each person brings everything they have to the mission. One person has keen vision. One person creates with skilled hands. One person is willing to do the legwork. Together, you and your family or friends are one body, capable of doing what a disconnected limb cannot.

Ask others for advice. See if they would be interested in joining you in a project that is much, much bigger than what you can accomplish on your own. Embrace the joy of moving toward something incredible, memorable, and worth tackling together.

Collaboration is held together by the mortar of love. Inviting others to join you doesn't mean that you are too weak to do it by yourself.

See yourselves as a group of people who work as one super hero.

God Himself is a synergistic super hero of three-as-one.

SEPTEMBER 26

READ OUT LOUD: James 2:22 (NIV)

You see that his faith and his actions were working together, and his faith was made complete by what he did.

There is synergistic power in small groups. People who share ideas and attempt things together can reach a higher level of creativity and spiritual productivity. Your involvement in church sets the example for collaboration that your children will follow.

But there is another type of integrated work your children can see in your home. What you *believe* about God has to show up in the way you live. Theory and practice have to operate in harmony.

- Do you believe your skill is a gift from God?
- Do you believe He has sent you to the mission field of your own workplace?
- Do you believe the people around you are made in the image of God, and He loves them?
- Do you believe that you are made in His image, and He loves you?
- Do you believe that you lead a one-person ministry of love?

There must be a synergy of theory and practice.
Belief needs feet.

SEPTEMBER 27

READ OUT LOUD: John 13:34 (NIV)

A new command I give you: Love one another. As I have loved you, so you must love one another.

You are to aim as high as you can.

The command to love is not calling you to a puny, half-hearted love. It is calling you to an all-out, extravagant love. Give the kind of love that Christ has given you.

That love is completely undeserved.

Actively look for someone who *doesn't deserve* to be treated well, and then treat them well anyway, in the name of Jesus.

REMEMBER A TIME WHEN SOMEONE GAVE YOU LOVE EVEN WHEN IT WAS UNDESERVED.

SEPTEMBER 28

READ OUT LOUD: 1 Corinthians 12:14-20 (CJB)

For indeed the body is not one part but many. If the foot says, "I'm not a hand, so I'm not part of the body," that doesn't make it stop being part of the body. And if the ear says, "I'm not an eye, so I'm not part of the body," that doesn't make it stop being part of the body. If the whole body were an eye, how could it hear? If it were all hearing, how could it smell? But as it is, God arranged each of the parts in the body exactly as He wanted them. Now if they were all just one part, where would the body be? But as it is, there are indeed many parts, yet just one body

God appreciates variety. He values diversity. He makes every person different, capable of different things. Your skills may seem small to you, but they are only small when you operate as an individual. You were designed to be plugged in, both to the Source of your power, which is God, and to a community where you can share that power through love. You will see the beautiful way God made you when you are a contributing part of something larger than yourself.

Stop asking what you were meant to do with your life.

Start asking what you were meant to do for the Kingdom.

When God brings the second question into focus, the first question will come into focus at the same time.

SEPTEMBER 29

READ OUT LOUD: James 1:5 (NIV)

If any of you lacks wisdom, you should ask God, who gives generously to all without finding fault, and it will be given to you.

You know where to go to get real wisdom.

No book or resource can offer what God can. He loves you, and He loves for you to ask Him for help.

If you normally pray in a certain posture—driving in the car, sitting at a table or in a comfortable chair—try a new posture today. Let your body reflect a new attitude in your heart.

Get on your knees to illustrate your submission to His instruction. Raise your hands high to show your celebration of His power. Bow your head to indicate your desire for His intellect.

As you kneel before Him, He will knight you with wisdom. As you lift your empty hands, He will fill them with the ability to accomplish all you need to do today. As you lower your head, He will anoint you once again with insight.

He has never turned away anyone who asked for more of Him.

SEPTEMBER 30

READ OUT LOUD: 3 John 1:8 (NIV)

We ought therefore to show hospitality to ... people so that we may work together for the truth.

You know why you often resented group work when you were growing up.

Overachievers do not like group work because they usually have to accomplish most of the work on the project. Underachievers do not like group work because they are pushed beyond their comfort zone.

Would it be possible to look at your next collaborative project as a chance to extend an invitation?

Collaboration is the greatest hospitality. It is inviting people into the creative room in your heart. In the same way that you may feel vulnerable when you bring someone into your home, you may feel vulnerable when you bring someone into your thought processes. What if they don't like it there? What if things are messier than they expected?

Observations of your own discomfort will help you be sensitive to other people on the project, as you *all* navigate the vulnerability that comes with collaboration.

OCTOBER

MEDITATIONS ON JOY

Always be joyful.

1 Thessalonians 5:16 (NLT)

OCTOBER 1

READ OUT LOUD: Nehemiah 8:10b (NIV)

... the joy of the Lord is your strength.

Joy is your strength so don't forget to play. Play when you have a day off, sure. But cultivate play throughout the week, as well.

There is a place for preparation, a place for planning ... and a place for *play*.

Unfortunately, the more you age, the less likely you are to play. But that doesn't make sense, because the longer you live in God's love, the more you love living.

What *is* play?

- It is uplifting and pure, never at anyone's expense.
- It is something you do with no motive other than joy and pleasure.
- It is making a game out of ordinary activities.
- It is approaching most interactions with a smile.
- It is playing hide-and-seek with God--He has hidden blessings throughout the day. You get to seek and find them.

Play is an important legacy to leave. The last thing adults should convey to the next generation is that life isn't fun.

OCTOBER 2

READ OUT LOUD: 2 Corinthians 5:17 (NIV)

Therefore, if anyone is in Christ, the new creation has come: The old has gone, the new is here!

There is always a chance to start over.

No matter what happened yesterday, no matter what happened this morning, no matter what happened five minutes ago, begin again *now*. Mistakes are a chance for a new direction.

When movie directors do not like what they are filming, they shout, "Cut! Retake!"

It is the same for you. Every *mis*take can be a *re*take.

This realization should bring you great joy. Jesus came to make a reset possible for you.

Don't pass up His offer to make all things—even *you*—brand new.

LIST THREE THINGS YOU ARE ASKING GOD TO MAKE NEW.

1. _____
2. _____
3. _____

OCTOBER 3

READ OUT LOUD: **Proverbs 18:21 (NIV)**

The tongue has the power of life and death, and those who love it will eat its fruit.

God created the universe by speaking. You are made in His image. That means that you can also create by speaking.

Examine the words that leave your mouth this week. Make sure each one of them is one you want to become something tangible in your life.

OCTOBER 4

READ OUT LOUD: Ephesians 5:4 (NLT)

Obscene stories, foolish talk, and coarse jokes—these are not for you. Instead, let there be thankfulness to God.

It has become common for Christians to jokingly advertise things like, "I love Jesus, but I cuss a little."

This casual attitude toward words is dangerous. God cares what you say and how you say it.

Everyone makes mistakes.

But everyone can also make a decision to honor the Lord with their mouths.

ASK GOD TO PURIFY YOUR SPEECH.

OCTOBER 5

READ OUT LOUD: 1 John 2:2 (MSG)

I write this, dear children, to guide you out of sin. But if anyone does sin, we have a Priest-Friend in the presence of the Father: Jesus Christ, righteous Jesus. When he served as a sacrifice for our sins, he solved the sin problem for good ...

It is easy to give in to guilt. But if you believe in Jesus and have committed your life to Him, then you are forever free from guilt because of His blood. Be aware that there is a difference between guilt and godly sorrow.

Godly sorrow is conviction. *Guilt* is condemnation.

Godly sorrow is healthy and will inspire spiritual growth. *Guilt* is unhealthy and will stop spiritual growth.

Godly sorrow is a negative feeling from the Holy Spirit about something you can change in the *present*. *Guilt* is a negative feeling from the enemy about something you can't change in the *past*.

Godly sorrow turns you toward tomorrow. *Guilt* turns you toward yesterday.

Godly sorrow brings change. *Guilt* brings chains.

Ask God to set you free from guilt today.
Because it's hard to feel joy in a jail.

OCTOBER 6

READ OUT LOUD: Psalm 27:1-3 (NLT)

The LORD is my light and my salvation—so why should I be afraid? The LORD is my fortress, protecting me from danger, so why should I tremble? When evil people come to devour me, when my enemies and foes attack me, they will stumble and fall. Though a mighty army surrounds me, my heart will not be afraid.

You are a God-carrier.

The Creator of the Universe, the Great and Mighty One, could never live in a dwelling made by clumsy human hands. Instead, He chooses to live in a dwelling made by His own holy hands. He lives in you. He goes with you wherever you go so anyone who comes against you, comes against Him.

You do not have to feel threatened or vulnerable. The Great Defender stands before you, behind you, with you, within you.

Let that bring a sense of joy as nothing else can.

OCTOBER 7

READ OUT LOUD: Galatians 5:1 (MSG)

Christ has set us free to live a free life. So take your stand! Never again let anyone put a harness of slavery on you.

As a believer, you are spiritually free, and your life is better for it. The only thing that should hold you back now is the gentle pressure of the Holy Spirit when He is cautioning you about an action or direction you are about to take.

God loves you passionately, and He wants to be loved passionately in return. Pray passionately. Worship passionately. Live the kind of passionate life that is only possible when you are free.

On the way to or from work today, play some music and praise God for your freedom in Christ. Give your all as you adore Him. There is nothing silly about pouring yourself out in pursuit of God. It is only silly *not* to pour yourself out in pursuit of Him.

God set your feet free because He wanted you to run to Him.

He set your hands free because He wanted you to lift them high.

OCTOBER 8

READ OUT LOUD: Matthew 6:33 (NLT)

Seek the Kingdom of God above all else, and live righteously, and he will give you everything you need.

Anticipation stays stuck in future-dreams.

"It will be different *then*," Anticipation says. "I'll have the right routines in place *then*. It will be easier *then*. I will be better and do better *then*. Might as well just wait until *then* to begin."

And all of the Kingdom work that God meant for you today is postponed until tomorrow. When you reach your anticipated tomorrow, the enemy's plan is to motivate you toward another anticipated tomorrow, and another and another, until you have lived so long for tomorrow that you no longer know how to live for today.

You may even be thinking that your real Kingdom work will begin later. But this *is* Kingdom work. Here and now. Consider that the people in your life may be there by design. It is likely that God wanted them to enjoy the spiritual gifts He put in you.

Why wait for *then*, when there is so much to do *now*?

Kingdom work is never about tomorrow because tomorrow never comes.

Work joyfully *today*.

OCTOBER 9

READ OUT LOUD: **Proverbs 4:13 (NIV)**

Hold on to instruction, do not let it go; guard it well, for it is your life.

Professional development is important. It may be inconvenient, but it is important, nonetheless. Try to face continuing education as a diamond mine. The more skill that miners have, the more treasure they can excavate, and the more they find joy in the process of excavation.

You are a skilled miner. You find treasure in your challenges all the time. There will be something meaningful for you to find in every one, even in mild challenges at work, like trainings and meetings. You know how to find value, so look for it. Find those few tiny gems that you can claim as your own.

If a work task feels dark to you, then do what you do best.
Mine for diamonds.

OCTOBER 10

READ OUT LOUD: Romans 12:12 (NLT)

Be joyful in hope, patient in affliction, faithful in prayer.

Hope is just a noun until it is activated by joy.
Then it becomes a verb, alive-and-kicking.

Joyless hope does nothing but imagine.
Joyful hope takes action.

And it prays.
Joy always prays.

WRITE DOWN FIVE THINGS YOU HOPE FOR. COMMIT TO PRAYING FOR THEM JOYFULLY.

1. _____
2. _____
3. _____
4. _____
5. _____

OCTOBER 11

READ OUT LOUD: James 1:2 (NLT)

Dear brothers and sisters, when troubles of any kind come your way, consider it an opportunity for great joy.

The easiest thing to do is to look at trouble as something that drains your joy.

Yet, God does something supernatural within the person who chooses to hold onto joy during times they feel like letting go. Trials are a great opportunity.

How can you hold onto joy?
Ask God to show you.

PRAY THIS SIMPLE PRAYER:

LORD, I WANT TO BELIEVE YOU WHEN YOU SAY THAT TROUBLE CAN BRING SUPERNATURAL JOY. PLEASE KEEP MY EYES AND EARS OPEN TODAY. I MAY NOT BE ABLE TO SEE JOY YET. BUT I DON'T WANT TO MISS IT.

OCTOBER 12

READ OUT LOUD: Philippians 4:4 (NLT)

Always be full of joy in the Lord. I say it again—rejoice!

The practice of joy is called rejoicing, and yes, it must be practiced.

Lead others in the practice of joy today:

WHAT ARE SIX THINGS YOU CAN DO TO PRACTICE JOY?

1. _____
2. _____
3. _____
4. _____
5. _____
6. _____

OCTOBER 13

READ OUT LOUD: John 16:24 (NLT)

You haven't done this before. Ask, using my name, and you will receive, and you will have abundant joy.

The name of Jesus is the most powerful tool in the world. You may know people who are desperately in need of help. Employ all the tools and resources at your disposal, but do not forget the most powerful one of all.

There is nothing like prayer in His name and in alignment with His will. When you are praying for others, you can easily know His will for them. He longs for all of His creation to be healed and whole. Anything less than wholeness is an opportunity for Him to display His glory in response to your prayers.

> Think of someone who is hurting.
> Bless that person in Jesus' name.
> Repeat as needed.

OCTOBER 14

READ OUT LOUD: Psalm 51:12 (NLT)

Restore to me the joy of your salvation, and make me willing to obey you.

It is a terrible feeling when you have been working on an important project, and then something happens to your computer ... and the document is gone! You realize too late that the recent revisions were not saved.

The horror is overwhelming. All of the work is lost. Nothing can be done.

BUT THEN!

You suddenly discover that you have a backup file, and all can be restored! Everything that went wrong can be made right again! Your work is saved after all!

That is what the joy of salvation feels like. You are not the only one who feels it. God feels it, too. He is your Creator. He has fashioned you wonderfully, putting marvelous attention into the lifelong project of making you into His image. He would be broken-hearted to see His masterpiece lost.

But you are *not* lost. You are saved. Forever.
Let the joy of your salvation permeate your life.

OCTOBER 15

READ OUT LOUD: **Revelation 21:5a (NLT)**

And the one sitting on the throne said, "Look, I am making everything new!"

In Genesis, the first picture of the Creator includes a glimpse into His studio. He is making new things in the Garden of Eden.

The moment He has an idea, He speaks. The moment He speaks, something *becomes*.

This is the God who knows your heart. He never stops the creative act of making you new.

Is the atmosphere starting to feel old and stale in your home? Let God speak into the room. Quietly read His Word aloud when you are alone.

He loves to create things *and* re-create things.

Let Him bring brand new joy within those four familiar walls.

THANK GOD FOR THREE THINGS ABOUT YOUR HOME THAT BRING YOU JOY.

1. _____
2. _____
3. _____

OCTOBER 16

READ OUT LOUD: Luke 2:10 (NIV)

But the angel said to them, "Do not be afraid. I bring you good news that will cause great joy for all the people."

One of the best things ever said about Jesus came in His birth announcement.

He was going to be *great joy for all the people*.

Not just *some* people.

All.

Everyone you meet can see a glimpse of the Greatest Joy because He lives in you. Show them the Lord in your words and deeds.

He is for *all*.

PRAY FOR SOMEONE WHO DOES NOT YET KNOW JESUS, THAT THEY WOULD ONE DAY MEET THEIR WONDERFUL SAVIOR.

OCTOBER 17

READ OUT LOUD: John 16:22 (NLT)

So you have sorrow now, but I will see you again; then you will rejoice, and no one can rob you of that joy.

Joy is a characteristic of the Fruit of the Spirit. It grows in you when you allow the Holy Spirit to reign in your life. The Fruit of the Spirit is incorruptible. Untouchable.

It is a common thing for people to say that Satan is stealing their joy.

Be careful that you do not give him credit for something he cannot do. It is not possible for him to steal your joy. He doesn't even *want* to. If he had ever wanted to steal someone's joy, it would have been Eve's. She was living in a perfect place. Few people experience Eve-level joy.

But what he stole from her was *not* her joy.

It was her trust in God's Word. That is what Satan wants to steal from you, too.

Hold fast to the Word today, and do not let your *trust* be stolen from you.

Don't worry about your joy.
Your joy is secure.

OCTOBER 18

READ OUT LOUD: **Romans 14:17 (NLT)**

For the Kingdom of God is not a matter of what we eat or drink, but of living a life of goodness and peace and joy in the Holy Spirit.

Some people get annoyed with others who are Pollyanna types, happy all day long. Those perpetually positive people could even be accused of not living in reality.

That perception of them couldn't be more wrong.

Joy is evidence of Jesus, and it is the principal descriptor of His Kingdom. The Kingdom is the highest reality, though most people in the world have no idea that this is true.

If you are the only Pollyanna-positive person you know, then so be it. Never give up the territory in your heart and mind that belongs to Jesus.

That is His Kingdom.
He is on the throne there, reigning with joy.

ASK GOD TO MAKE YOU RESILIENT IN THE FACE OF CRITICISM FROM OTHERS.

OCTOBER 19

READ OUT LOUD: **Psalm 43:4 (NLT)**

There I will go to the altar of God, to God—the source of all my joy.

Discouragement and fear will find you.

You *never* have to go looking for them.

Hope and joy will hide from you.

You *always* have to hunt for them.

If the day has drained you dry, if you feel broken, down, and exhausted, then run to God to refill you. He is the source of your joy.

Like a rushing river, He offers an endless supply for you to drink.

LIST FOUR THINGS THAT YOU ARE THANKFUL FOR TODAY.

1. _____
2. _____
3. _____
4. _____

OCTOBER 20

READ OUT LOUD: Romans 15:13 (NLT)

I pray that God, the source of hope, will fill you completely with joy and peace because you trust in him. Then you will overflow with confident hope through the power of the Holy Spirit.

How can you receive joy from the Lord? Is it just the product of coming to Him in praise instead of in complaint? Is it the mark of coming to Him with thanksgiving instead of with constant requests?

Yes, come to God in praise.

Yes, come to Him with thanksgiving.

But joy is the result of coming to Him *just because you trust Him.*

COMMIT TO TRUSTING GOD IN THREE AREAS THAT HAVE BEEN WEIGHING ON YOUR MIND.

1. _____
2. _____
3. _____

OCTOBER **21**

READ OUT LOUD: Psalm 118:24 (NLT)

This is the day the Lord has made. We will rejoice and be glad in it.

There are some days that are so difficult it is a challenge to feel any joy. On those days, it might help to begin the process of *feeling* joy by first *finding* joy in your circumstances.

RIGHT IN THE MIDDLE OF YOUR DAY—MAYBE DURING YOUR BREAKFAST OR LUNCH—SIT DOWN AND START A SIMPLE LIST. ARE THERE SOME THINGS THAT YOU CAN *COUNT* AS JOY ... EVEN THOUGH YOU MAY NOT BE ABLE TO *FEEL* THEM AS JOY JUST YET? ENUMERATE YOUR REASONS FOR JOY. LIST AS MANY AS YOU CAN.

1. _____
2. _____
3. _____
4. _____
5. _____
6. _____
7. _____

OCTOBER 22

READ OUT LOUD: Isaiah 55:11-12 (NLT)

[My word] will accomplish all I want it to, and it will prosper everywhere I send it. You will live in joy and peace.

The power of God's Word is beyond understanding. He sent it to reveal Himself to us, but He also sent it to give us power.

When His Word goes out, it produces His will: joy and peace. Plant seeds of joy and peace in your home by continuing to read Scripture out loud there.

Other people do not always need to *hear* His Word to be blessed by it.

God's miracle-working voice still speaks.

Let your family and friends receive the blessing through your mouth.

LOCATE A BIBLE VERSE THAT YOU REALLY NEED. WRITE IT OUT HERE. READ IT OUT LOUD WHEN YOU ARE ALONE.

_____

_____

_____

_____

_____

OCTOBER 23

READ OUT LOUD: Proverbs 10:28 (NIV)

The prospect of the righteous is joy, but the hopes of the wicked come to nothing.

It is always easy to imagine a disaster. You can picture the whole thing going south easier than you can visualize it working in your favor.

Your hope will not disappoint you. Know that there is joy in your future, even if you can't envision it now. You may not be able to see how the things you hope for will come to pass, but by entrusting your desires to God, you are ensuring that there will be joy, no matter the outcome.

Anything you keep in your hands is vulnerable, even though you feel secure.

Anything you place in His hands is secure, even though you feel vulnerable.

SIT FOR A MOMENT TODAY AND LIST YOUR GREATEST DESIRES AT WORK AND AT HOME. WHAT DO YOU WANT MOST? BY LISTING THEM HERE, YOU ARE LETTING THEM GO AND PLACING THEM IN GOD'S HANDS.

1. _____
2. _____
3. _____

OCTOBER 24

READ OUT LOUD: Psalm 33:20-21 (MSG)

We're depending on God; he's everything we need. What's more, our hearts brim with joy since we've taken for our own his holy name.

There is no joy like that of a couple on their wedding day.

Only that kind of joy would cause people to take on new roles and join families. In most cases, the bride and groom share a last name. The two are no longer two separate ones, but *two-as-one*.

This is the kind of joy you bring everywhere you go. You are no longer alone. You have invited the Lord into your heart and have surrendered to Him. You have taken the name of Jesus as your own. Now you are forever two-as-one. And as you draw near to the One you love, you are empowered and protected.

Your joy can be wedding-day joy.

LIST THREE THINGS THAT BELONG TO YOU SIMPLY BECAUSE YOU ARE ONE WITH CHRIST.

1. _____
2. _____
3. _____

OCTOBER 25

READ OUT LOUD: Psalm 4:7 (NLT)

You have given me greater joy than those who have abundant harvests of grain and new wine.

The temptation to compare yourself to others is great. When you compare your life to others, perhaps you feel envious. You might compare your skill. You could compare your relationships, resources, or health at any time and feel you have come up short.

This way of measuring does not generate joy. If anything, it works against it. The more you focus on what others have, the less you focus on the power of God within you. He loves you deeply. He longs to see your success. He will help you anytime you ask. He is fully able to work miracles on your behalf. The Creator of the universe stands near and ready.

Now, *that's* something to compare.

And you will find nothing else comes close to matching the majesty of that truth.

OCTOBER 26

READ OUT LOUD: Psalm 71:23 (NKJV)

My lips shall greatly rejoice when I sing to You, And my soul, which You have redeemed.

Your spirit and soul are two different things. The spirit is the part of you that communes with God, sensing His presence and feeling His peace beyond understanding. It is the part of you that is eternal.

The soul is made up of your mind, will, and emotions. Your spirit rules over your soul, and your soul rules over your body.

This is how you access joy:

First, your spirit instructs your soul to bless the Lord and trust, even though the horizon looks frightening. Then, your soul instructs your body to praise God and sing, even when you don't have any energy.

Your spirit tells your soul to *believe* differently.
Your soul tells your body to *behave* differently.

OCTOBER 27

READ OUT LOUD: Psalm 100:1 (MSG)

On your feet now—applaud God! Bring a gift of laughter, sing yourselves into His presence.

The book of Psalms is filled with anguish and fear and cries of desperation. Even so, on every page there is praise. Acknowledging God seems to transport King David from trouble to triumph within the same sentence.

Praise is the chariot that carries us into joyful territory.

God *has* never failed.
He *will* never fail.

IF YOU'RE STRUGGLING TO FIND A WAY TO PRAISE, START HERE. WRITE DOWN SEVEN TIMES HE TOOK GOOD CARE OF YOU.

1. _____
2. _____
3. _____
4. _____
5. _____
6. _____
7. _____

OCTOBER 28

READ OUT LOUD: Isaiah 29:19 (NLT)

The humble will be filled with fresh joy from the Lord.

There is a connection between humility and joy. Part of that is a spiritual connection that we cannot see or imagine. But there is also a connection that is rooted in the physical world.

Some people will go to great lengths to make themselves look good. Perhaps this is done out of fear. They want to make sure they are known as a valuable asset in their professional lives. Maybe they take most of the credit for a collaborative effort. Maybe they boast about their results. Or they want to be known as satisfied and successful in their personal lives. Maybe they over share about their relationships and name-drop. Maybe they paint a picture of having it all together in their home.

Do not be fooled. There is never any joy in working that hard to look good.

Let your work speak for itself.
Find joy in simple humility.

THANK GOD FOR ONE OF YOUR PROFESSIONAL OR PERSONAL ACCOMPLISHMENTS, WHETHER LARGE OR SMALL.

_____

_____

OCTOBER 29

READ OUT LOUD: Matthew 25:21 (NKJV)

Well done, good and faithful servant; you were faithful over a few things, I will make you ruler over many things. Enter into the joy of your lord.

You may work under an employer who brings you great joy. You may work under one who makes the day miserable. As much as possible, remember that your true Master is the Lord.

He is the One you must seek to please. He is the One who holds your reward. You have been entrusted with a series of small tasks in your lifetime. If you dedicate all you do to Him, He will increase your opportunities and responsibilities. Do not disdain the days of small assignments. These are the stones that pave the way to great landscapes.

God possesses unending joy.
And He longs to share it with faithful servants.

IF GOD IS YOUR TRUE MASTER, THEN SPEND A MOMENT ASKING HIM TO REVIEW AND HELP YOU IMPROVE YOUR EFFORTS.

OCTOBER 30

READ OUT LOUD: **Psalm 126:6 (NIV)**

Those who go out weeping, carrying seed to sow, will return with songs of joy, carrying sheaves with them.

Everything you plant will become a harvest.

When you first begin speaking encouragement into friends and family members, you may not notice growth. Yet, if you consistently plant God's Word and your confident hope into their hearts, eventually you will not be able to contain the fruit that it produces.

Be aware that it may take some time to uproot what others have planted in them.

Pray and let God do the work of weeding while you are planting good seed.

IN A GENERAL WAY, PRAY FOR THOSE WHO MAY NEED THE LORD TO DO SOME WEEDING IN THEIR LIVES.

OCTOBER 31

READ OUT LOUD: Zephaniah 3:17 (NKJV)

The Lord your God in your midst, The Mighty One, will save; He will rejoice over you with gladness, He will quiet you with His love, He will rejoice over you with singing.

Just when you feel that you are the one who is doing all of the encouraging, stop and allow the Lord to encourage *you*.

He delights in you.
He is with you now.
He is singing over you.
Quiet your heart so you can hear it.

Come to Him and rest.
Listen to your Father's joyful lullaby.

THINK CREATIVELY AND IMAGINATIVELY. WRITE OUT THE CHORUS OF GOD'S LULLABY FOR YOU.

_____

_____

_____

_____

_____

NOVEMBER

MEDITATIONS ON PEACE

You will keep in perfect peace those whose minds are steadfast, because they trust in you.

Isaiah 26:3 (NIV)

NOVEMBER 1

READ OUT LOUD: **Matthew 13:31-32 (NIV)**

The kingdom of heaven is like a mustard seed, which a man took and planted in his field. Though it is the smallest of all seeds, yet when it grows, it is the largest of garden plants and becomes a tree, so that the birds come and perch in its branches.

Autumn is the season of discovery. Crisp breezes bring change. The horizon is electric with variety. So the earth conserves energy in anticipation of the coming cold.

Winter is the season of distraction. Christmas excitement brings frenzy. Special activities are electric with variety. So the wise person conserves energy in anticipation of the coming crazy.

Now is the time to plant deep. Seeds must be buried far under the surface in order to withstand the frost of winter. The seeds lie dormant there, and no progress can be seen, but when the weather warms, every stunning bloom will open to the sun.

You know that growth and change take time. But be at peace. Soon enough, beauty will emerge.

Plan for it now.
Plant for it now.

NOVEMBER 2

READ OUT LOUD: Philippians 4:8 (NLT)

Fix your thoughts on what is true, and honorable, and right, and pure, and lovely, and admirable. Think about things that are excellent and worthy of praise.

Most days are laced with both good and bad news. You cannot choose the timing of the news. You cannot choose the content of the news. But you *can* choose the volume of the news in your head. You *can* choose how often you hit repeat.

It is so easy for you to listen to the worst reports at deafening decibels and rewind them far too often. This is not necessary. The loudness at which you hear that information will not affect the outcome. Also, the frequency with which you think about that information will not affect the outcome.

You can maximize your worries or minimize them. Try to turn down the dial. This is not to suggest that ignoring a situation will solve it. Some things must be addressed in real time. But if you heard some positive news today, you will not hold onto it unless you are intentional. You will start replaying it less and less and then not at all.

If you let Positivity go, it will depart without a whisper of protest, but Negativity will nag to be heard.

It won't *let you* let it go.

NOVEMBER 3

READ OUT LOUD: Psalm 30:5b (NIV)

... weeping may stay for the night, but rejoicing comes with the morning.

Learning how to think positively is a big part of developing character. A smile has more power than you know. Use a smile to turn around a difficult situation.

This is not smiling from manipulation. It is not smiling from sarcasm. It is smiling from optimism. Smiling comes from a deep supply of security and peace. Smiling comes from a genuine belief that things can change.

The first thing to change in a situation—always—must be your attitude. Don't wait for peace to come. Make a choice to remain at peace.

Optimism is not an unrealistic fairy tale. It is not a crazy idea. Hope is real and true. Thinking positively helps you find pathways, solutions, possibilities you would have missed if you had given up.

> There will be a good outcome, even yet.
> Smile and let your face say it all.

NOVEMBER 4

READ OUT LOUD: 2 Thessalonians 3:16 (NLT)

Now may the Lord of peace himself give you his peace at all times and in every situation. The Lord be with you all.

It is unnatural to stay calm in an emergency. The fight or flight response is instinctual. When an alarm sounds, when things go wrong, we want to run away. Our hearts race, and our feet cannot stay at a steady pace. But fleeing abruptly can increase the danger.

Panic invites peril.

Peace invites protection.

Fear may be a first response, but it is not a constructive response. You purposefully collect your things and exit the building in a fire drill. In the same way, be purposeful when things go wrong at work or at home.

That interaction was a disaster? That attempt to connect didn't work? It's getting worse?

Pretend it is a fire drill. Purposefully collect your thoughts and exit the room. Respectfully step away and catch your breath. Think how this crazy situation could become a redeemable moment. The resurrection power of the Lord can breathe into a lifeless situation.

Pray. Then re-enter the room.

And bring the love of Jesus with you.

NOVEMBER 5

READ OUT LOUD: Proverbs 14:23 (NIV)

All hard work brings a profit, but mere talk leads only to poverty.

Rain is as important as sunlight. Every day's weather is not the same. Neither is the climate in your home. Everyone meets challenges. View those challenges as the necessary downpours that make way for brighter blooms.

A peaceful heart can navigate anything. And it is artful navigation in bad weather that allows for real growth. Sunny days *will* come. Until they do, work hard in the rain. All parts of the process are part of the progress.

> A lot of people *talk* about perseverance.
> Only the faithful truly persevere.

HEAVENLY FATHER, HELP ME PERSEVERE IN THE AREA OF _____ TODAY.

NOVEMBER 6

READ OUT LOUD: **Proverbs 15:1 (NLT)**

A gentle answer deflects anger, but harsh words make tempers flare.

Every person who talks with you is carrying the memories of their past. This is why some people communicate with smiles and encouraging words. But this is also why some people communicate with scowls and accusing words. If something or someone has reminded them of an event that was humiliating or painful, then they may be affected ... and take it out on you.

Maybe they felt powerless as a child to express themselves to that teacher or parent. Now, every time they have a chance to communicate with someone, they want to exert the power they never could when they were young. No wonder they come into your presence prepared to unleash pent-up self-defense. They may have been stewing over *what they wish they had said* for thirty years. They may not even realize that these past emotions compel them in the present.

It is not fair for you to be mistreated for someone else's mistakes. And it is not your responsibility to repair someone else's mistakes.

But if you can show compassion and speak peace into a troubled heart, always take the opportunity to do so.

NOVEMBER 7

READ OUT LOUD: Isaiah 53:5b (NIV)

...the punishment that brought us peace was on him, and by his wounds we are healed.

As an exercise in cultivating peace, try agreeing with Truth in a new way today.

Each and every time you do not feel at peace, repeat this sentence:

It is finished.

Jesus died to give you peace. The quest for peace is over.

By reciting these words of Jesus, you will be instructing your heart to align with what God has already said.

LIST FIVE THINGS IN YOUR LIFE THAT ARE FINISHED BECAUSE GOD SAYS THEY ARE.

1. _____
2. _____
3. _____
4. _____
5. _____

NOVEMBER 8

READ OUT LOUD: Proverbs 21:1-2 (NLT)

The king's heart is like a stream of water directed by the Lord; he guides it wherever he pleases. People may be right in their own eyes, but the Lord examines their heart.

When you feel some resistance from others, try not to retaliate, even if you think they are wrong. It can be tempting to come back with a quick retort, but this is not effective in the long-run ... or the short-run, for that matter. How impressive is it when someone has a quick comeback for you? How much do you feel like listening to that person the next time he or she speaks?

If you need to appeal a decision or behavior, appeal with dignity. Then if your request is not heard or heeded, behave graciously. Let it be evident that your peace runs deep.

Show honor for the authoritative position, even if you do not feel like showing honor to the authoritative person. Show respect for an administrative role, even if you do not have respect for the one who fills it.

Then take your concern to the One who is above *their* heads.

NOVEMBER 9

READ OUT LOUD: Isaiah 30:15b (NIV)

In repentance and rest is your salvation, in quietness and trust is your strength ...

A hectic schedule can easily get the best of you.

Some people say, "If I am not busy, something feels 'off.' I prefer to have a lot on my plate."

Yes, busyness can be energizing. Busyness can be healthy. But busyness also can be avoidance. It is possible for busyness to mask something that needs to change.

Every time you took an academic test, your teacher cautioned you by pointing out, "Now might be a good time to slow down and check your work." Teachers know that if their students go too fast, they are liable to overlook an error they could have avoided.

In this case, what was true then is true now.

Are you moving so quickly that you could make some careless errors right now? Set aside some time—even just fifteen minutes—to look at your life and re-evaluate the way you spend your day. Quiet rest is not inferior to busyness. Peace is not inferior to pace. The key is balance.

If your patience is being put to the test, now might be a good time to slow down and check your work.

NOVEMBER 10

READ OUT LOUD: Isaiah 26:3 (NIV)

You will keep in perfect peace those whose minds are steadfast, because they trust in you.

The longer a you do anything, the less planning seems necessary. You already know what needs to come next. You know what you are doing. You know where you are going, and you might feel that pausing to plan hinders you sometimes. It takes precious minutes that you could spend doing other things. Things that seem more important.

Never underestimate the power of preparation, though. Your expertise does not *replace* a plan; it makes you uniquely equipped to *execute* that plan.

Preparation brings peace.

Think through the obstacles. Pray through the possibilities.

Let God guide your mind now, so that later, He can guide your hands.

PRAY FOR GOD'S PEACE TO POUR INTO YOUR HOME AND WORK.

NOVEMBER 11

READ OUT LOUD: 2 Peter 3:5 (MSG)

They conveniently forget that long ago all the galaxies and this very planet were brought into existence out of watery chaos by God's word.

Slow down. Be at peace. Reduce the number of things you try to do at one time, in one day. The more that multitasking becomes a habit of the modern world, the more we wander into the dangerous territory of chaos. Our thought patterns become scattered, and the state of our homes and relationships follow close behind. Soon enough, there is a gaping loss of meaning, as all things slowly return to their original state. Chaos is entropy, and chaos is empty.

You do not have to live in chaos.

In the beginning, God saw the original chaos and spoke LIGHT.

He spoke LIFE.
He spoke ORDER.
He spoke BOUNDARY.
He spoke MEANING.

As often as you can, read God's Word out loud; it still has the power to do what it did *in the beginning*.

NOVEMBER 12

READ OUT LOUD: John 7:38 (NKJV)

He who believes in Me, as the Scripture has said, out of his heart will flow rivers of living water.

One who is dehydrated cannot find peace. She is always searching for a way to slake her thirst.

The next time your heart feels a thirst or emptiness, ask the Lord to fill you with an awareness of Him. The Holy Spirit flows like living water out of the heart of every believer. If you feel an ache, it may be because the stress and bustle of your daily work has made you forget the Spirit's quiet, flowing presence within you.

Drink for yourself first. Then you will be able to refresh others.

TAKE A MOMENT TO WRITE ABOUT SOMETHING THAT IS MAKING YOUR HEART FEEL "THIRSTY." ALSO WRITE ABOUT WHAT WOULD MAKE YOU FEEL REFRESHED.

NOVEMBER 13

READ OUT LOUD: Psalm 27:10 (NLT)

Even if my father and mother abandon me, the LORD will hold me close.

It doesn't matter how much acceptance God shows you. If you do not choose to receive that acceptance, the critical circuit of love is not complete.

But the moment that you do receive your acceptance, there is a surge of peace that will be unequaled in your life.

Set a timer for three minutes and give yourself the gift of meditation today. Before you begin, say a quick prayer that God will guide your heart and mind and use those minutes to fill you with peace.

As you meditate, picture a beautiful dinner table. Imagine every detail of the centerpiece and place settings. Think about the music in the background and the dishes of delicious food. Hear the laughter. See the smiles. Feel the joy. Everyone is waiting for one beloved guest. Now imagine that *you* walk in. The noble Host stands from His place at the head of the table to greet you. All of His guests are delighted you have come.

It is God's banquet.
And He says you are accepted here.

NOVEMBER 14

READ OUT LOUD: Revelation 3:8 (NLT)

I know all the things you do, and I have opened a door for you that no one can close. You have little strength, yet you obeyed my word and did not deny me.

Do not let the enemy convince you that he can close a door that the Lord has opened. God says you are accepted. That is truth. Anything else is a lie.

Both lies and truth require belief. Does it shock you that lies are easier to believe than truth? That may be a matter of exposure. When your mind is idle, it will go to the "screen saver" idea that you have been exposed to most often. Many voices in the world tell you that you are not good enough, fast enough, pretty enough, knowledgeable enough, experienced enough, young enough ...

So many voices will tell you that you are rejected.

The only voice that says you are enough is God's. He says you are accepted as you are. If you are not exposing yourself to truth as often as you are being exposed to the enemy's lies, then lies will become the screen saver during those moments of "down time" in your mind.

God has brought you to Himself in peace.
Refuse to believe any other message.

NOVEMBER 15

READ OUT LOUD: James 1:5-7 (MSG)

If you don't know what you're doing, pray to the Father. He loves to help. You'll get his help, and won't be condescended to when you ask for it. Ask boldly, believingly, without a second thought. People who 'worry their prayers' are like wind-whipped waves. Don't think you're going to get anything from the Master that way, adrift at sea, keeping all your options open.

God understands *complex* things—the creation of the universe, the procreation of life.

These are the things humans try to over-simplify.

God wants *simple* things—a relationship with His children, a prayer-conversation.

These are the things humans try to over-complicate.

You don't have to have everything figured out today. If you want clarity, just ask.

He will lead you with peace.

ASK THE LORD TO HELP YOU UNDERSTAND THREE DIFFICULT CONCEPTS, SPIRITUAL OR OTHERWISE.

1. _____
2. _____
3. _____

NOVEMBER 16

READ OUT LOUD: John 5:17 (NLT)

But Jesus replied, "My Father is always working and so am I."

If you are conscientious, you desire to work—to provide for your family, to stay involved in the church, to take on areas of leadership and service. Yet, the more you pile on your plate, the less effective you become in any of those endeavors.

Maybe if you let go of one of your projects, it will open a place for someone else to step up for the first time. Maybe it will give you a chance to get away and spend time with God.

Deliberately resting is like sending Peace an invitation to come to your house.

THANK GOD FOR FIVE ACTIVITIES THAT BRING A FEELING OF PEACE TO YOU.

1. _____
2. _____
3. _____
4. _____
5. _____

NOVEMBER 17

READ OUT LOUD: Psalm 4:8 (NIV)

In peace I will lie down and sleep, for you alone, Lord, make me dwell in safety.

Do not try to overwork. Give your best effort to God, as if it were your loaves and fish. Give Him what you have today. Then let Jesus handle the multiplication. Oh, His miraculous math!

Choosing Sabbath rest is the perfect way to partner with God. Give Him what you have this week, then just stop.

While you rest, He will do the rest.

PRAY A BLESSING OF REST OVER YOUR NEXT HOLIDAY OR BREAK. PRAY A BLESSING OF REST OVER YOUR NEXT WEEKEND. PRAY A BLESSING OF REST OVER YOUR NEXT AFTERNOON AND EVENING.

NOVEMBER 18

READ OUT LOUD: **Romans 14:19 (NKJV)**

Therefore let us pursue the things which make for peace and the things by which one may edify another.

Peace is not an accident, although it always *seems* effortless. While you are experiencing peace, there is not a lot tugging or tearing at you.

However, if you feel peace in a room, it is because someone pursued it and fought for it. Sometimes you will have to be that person pursuing peace and fighting for it. Others may never know that the peace they sense in your presence is something you have worked hard to attain.

Peace is the result of a battle.

THANK GOD FOR FOUR PLACES YOU LOVE TO GO BECAUSE YOU SENSE PEACE WHEN YOU ARE THERE.

1. _____
2. _____
3. _____
4. _____

NOVEMBER 19

READ OUT LOUD: Isaiah 32:17 (NKJV)

The work of righteousness will be peace. And the effect of righteousness, quietness and assurance forever.

Keeping a clear conscience doesn't win you any ticket into heaven or any more love from God. Both God's love and a room in His home are free gifts to those who accept His Son.

But there is a peace that comes when you operate from integrity and do what is right. You were created in the image of God, and it just feels good when you do what He would do.

The person who chooses to lie or cheat or act unfairly brings unnecessary worries into his life. That person is always on edge, wondering whether she will be found out. But the one who lives righteously lives with a peaceful heart.

When you deal with people who do not value integrity, it can be discouraging, but try not to let yourself think *they* are better off than *you* are. In the end, they forfeit peace, and you keep it.

Let the reward of peace be a motivator in your decision-making.

NOVEMBER 20

READ OUT LOUD: Isaiah 32:18 (NKJV)

My people will live in peaceful dwelling places, in secure homes, in undisturbed places of rest.

God desires for His people to be set apart, to stand out as having different motivations and different value systems. People tend to generalize the term *value system* to mean *morality*. In part, this is what it means. Yet, values are whatever a person considers to be of great value or worth. A Christian is motivated, less by a different set of rules, and more by a different definition of reward.

The rewards can be difficult to see, sometimes. Often, they must be *felt*. One such reward is a peaceful home. Believers who put all of their trust in the Lord receive a wonderful sense of security. They have placed themselves in capable Hands. Even people who do not know Jesus might be able to recognize a subtle difference in the home of a committed follower of Christ.

The same can be said of the office or workplace of a believer. It is possible for the peace that surrounds you to act as a quiet witness of your faith. When clients or colleagues walk into your space, they will notice the change in the atmosphere.

Yours is a faith that can be felt.

NOVEMBER 21

READ OUT LOUD: Proverbs 17:14 (NLT)

Starting a quarrel is like opening a floodgate, so stop before a dispute breaks out.

When something has been nagging at you, you might want to go back and revisit the situation. Perhaps someone said something that hurt your feelings or seemed accusatory, and you want to straighten out the misunderstanding.

Before you go back to address an offense, consider the possibility of just moving forward instead. It could be worth covering the wound so that you don't make things worse by reopening it.

If you don't let a problem go, you might be letting it grow.

Ask the Holy Spirit if He is leading you to revisit a disagreement or to do nothing. Every situation is different, but all situations can be bathed in forgiveness.

> Sometimes *action* will bring about peace.
> Sometimes *inaction* will.
> God will help you know the difference.

IS THERE AN AREA WHERE GOD IS URGING YOU TO ACT OR NOT ACT? WHAT IS THE HOLY SPIRIT SAYING RIGHT NOW?

_____

_____

NOVEMBER 22

READ OUT LOUD: Isaiah 48:18 (NIV)

If only you had paid attention to my commands, your peace would have been like a river, your well-being like the waves of the sea.

The biblical commands that feel as if they are hindering you are just seat belts.

They keep you safe.

You are keenly aware of this because any regulations you create to restrain others are meant for their safety too. When people pull and push against them, it is because they don't understand the purpose behind the rules.

View this rebellion with gentle and knowing eyes. At times, you act the same.

God's standards do not keep you from living your life. They keep you safe so that you *can* live your life.

THANK GOD FOR TWO OF HIS COMMANDS THAT HAVE KEPT YOU SAFE OVER THE YEARS.

1. _____
2. _____

NOVEMBER 23

READ OUT LOUD: Matthew 10:19-20 (MSG)

And don't worry about what you'll say or how you'll say it. The right words will be there; the Spirit of your Father will supply the words.

People may not understand the stressors you experience. At times, you may feel as if you are on stage, and everyone in the audience is watching you, expecting you to advance the scene. But you just freeze.

Let it bring you peace to know that God will guide your mouth, if you let Him. When you come to a thought that is challenging to convey, when you hit a wall of exhaustion, when you meet resistance, the Lord will help you find the words at just the right time.

If you forget your lines, God will whisper your cue at the corner of the stage.

NOVEMBER 24

READ OUT LOUD: John 14:26 (NLT)

But when the Father sends the Advocate as my representative—that is, the Holy Spirit—he will teach you everything and will remind you of everything I have told you.

Read the Bible as often as possible.

You do not have to have many passages memorized in order to benefit from the Word.

Part of the Holy Spirit's job is to bring Jesus' teachings to your mind at the right times.

If you read, He will supply what you need.

IS THERE A BIBLE VERSE THAT YOU WOULD LIKE TO MEMORIZE? WRITE IT OUT HERE AND ON A STICKY NOTE THAT YOU WILL SEE DAILY.

_____

_____

_____

_____

_____

_____

_____

NOVEMBER 25

READ OUT LOUD: Galatians 1:3 (NLT)

May God the Father and our Lord Jesus Christ give you grace and peace.

You belong to the Kingdom of God, and you carry peace with you.

It is possible for you, in the Holy Spirit's power, to dispense peace wherever you go. Greet people in peace. Give them a sense of peace when you part ways. If you do, people may receive a gift from you that they have never received from anyone else.

Please don't let anyone leave your presence, wondering if you are still angry with them. Make peace before you part ways. Even if a day was rough, always take a moment to reassure that person that tomorrow will be a better day. Move toward reconciliation, even if you can't see how you are going to get there.

Peace deserves your protection.

PRAY A BLESSING OF PEACE OVER YOUR RELATIONSHIPS.

NOVEMBER 26

READ OUT LOUD: Philippians 4:6-7 (MSG)

Don't fret or worry. Instead of worrying, pray. Let petitions and praises shape your worries into prayers, letting God know your concerns. Before you know it, a sense of God's wholeness, everything coming together for good, will come and settle you down. It's wonderful what happens when Christ displaces worry at the center of your life.

Anxiety froths in your mind and in your heart like a scientific experiment gone wrong. It spills over the brim of what you can safely hold in your thoughts at one time.

Anxiety is tomorrow happening *today*.

Anxiety is the next five minutes happening *right now*.

Of course you cannot contain it! It's too much! For many people, anxiety is synonymous with worry, but not for everyone. If anxiety resonates in a different way with you, Bible verses about worry and over-concern will still have a powerful effect.

If there is a moment in your day when anxiety hits, try barely whispering a Scripture under your breath. Simply repeating God's Word makes His presence tangible. And His presence always brings peace.

It acts as a soothing "base" to the acidic reaction of anxious thoughts.

NOVEMBER 27

READ OUT LOUD: Ecclesiastes 3:8 (NLT)

There is ... a time to love and a time to hate. A time for war and a time for peace.

Two communicators can attempt to convey the same concept, but the one with a keen sense of timing will be twice as effective. It is difficult to train a person to know when to shift the discussion, when to lengthen the explanation, and when to cut either one short. It is hard to describe when a conversation should be abandoned or how to deliver corrections effectively.

God knows that there are a lot of ways communication can take a wrong turn.

He will give you the peace to walk His way.

ASK THE LORD TO PERFECT YOUR SENSE OF TIMING.

NOVEMBER 28

READ OUT LOUD: Matthew 5:9 (NLT)

God blesses those who work for peace, for they will be called the children of God.

Be a peacemaker. A peacemaker is a peace-*generator*.

Generate peace in the room. Work for it. Try to understand before being understood. Treat people better than they treat you.

In some cases, a consistently kind response can de-escalate an agitated person.

But only if it is genuine.

You don't have to win. Being right cannot be your goal. Resolving conflict is your goal.

When that happens, both of you win.
And that is what you really want, after all.

COMMIT A RECENT DISAGREEMENT TO THE LORD.

_____
_____
_____
_____
_____

NOVEMBER 29

READ OUT LOUD: John 20:19b (NIV)

Jesus came and stood among them and said, "Peace be with you!"

Jesus wants you to have peace; He is not withholding it.

He calls it out.

He pours it over you.

In a world that is hurried and harried, nothing goes against the grain more than someone who is at peace. Today, notice when things go wrong, or tension rises. These are areas where you can make a difference in the lives of those around you by calling out peace the way Jesus does.

You do not have to say much.

One way to pour peace over a situation is by choosing to display the posture of peace.

HOW DOES A PEACEFUL PERSON SOUND? WHAT DOES A PEACEFUL PERSON LOOK LIKE?

NOVEMBER 30

READ OUT LOUD: Isaiah 54:13 (NIV)

All your children will be taught by the Lord, and great will be their peace.

The greatest prayer you can pray for children is that they will be taught by the Lord. Ask Him to teach them *through* you. He understands their hearts better than anyone, and He can see what they need to learn.

Your *indirect influence* in their lives will never end, but your *direct influence* will end at some point.

As you pray for young people, extend your blessing into their futures.

PRAY THAT HE WILL INCREASE THEIR PEACE.

DECEMBER

MEDITATIONS ON PATIENCE

But if we hope for what we do not yet have, we wait for it patiently.

Romans 8:25 (NIV)

DECEMBER 1

READ OUT LOUD: Proverbs 22:29 (NIV)

Do you see someone skilled in their work? They will serve before kings; they will not serve before officials of low rank.

They asked you for a solution again.

Many people in your circle swivel to face you when there is a problem. If they need an answer, they know where to find one.

If you sense that your colleagues and friends are turning to you more often, it is because they are. You have proven yourself to be someone who keeps a can-do attitude. If you are feeling overworked, you can ask that the load be shared. But you don't have to dread the next time that someone turns to you expectantly. The Holy Spirit has prepared you with special insight and skill. Why are you surprised that other people can see it shining in you?

You have creativity burning in your heart, and there is always a coal of it glowing in there somewhere. So try not to see requests as a burden.

Receive their expectations with patience. They are doing you a favor. They are stoking the embers of inventiveness in you.

Let it burn.

DECEMBER 2

READ OUT LOUD: 1 Corinthians 10:13 (NLT)

The temptations in your life are no different from what others experience. And God is faithful. He will not allow the temptation to be more than you can stand. When you are tempted, he will show you a way out so that you can endure.

Prepare your heart and spirit now. The deepest parts of you will be drawn out by difficulty at least once this year, and you want to be ready.

When circumstances become demanding, that can be a good thing. Have patience and persevere. Pressure releases the fragrance and essence of who you are on the inside.

The only way to get juice is by squeezing the orange.

THANK GOD FOR DIFFICULTIES. PRAISE HIM THAT HE IS ABLE TO BRING GOOD OUT OF PAIN, EVEN WHEN YOU CAN'T SEE HOW.

DECEMBER 3

READ OUT LOUD: Matthew 17:20 (NLT)

"You don't have enough faith," Jesus told them. "I tell you the truth, if you had faith even as small as a mustard seed, you could say to this mountain, 'Move from here to there,' and it would move. Nothing would be impossible."

Small investments of effort make a big difference over time. Small investments of encouragement make a big difference over time, too.

Remember that people grow when they receive incremental nourishment: small affirmations repeated *every day*.

A potted plant needs water—in incremental amounts—*every day*. Or at least every few days.

Six month's worth of water poured on a plant all at one time will drown it. Six month's worth of encouragement poured on a person all at one time will not be as effective as daily or weekly encouragement in incremental amounts.

Be patient.

You don't have to make a gigantic effort to raise their spirits. Make affirmation frequent and make it small. Do it faithfully.

> Affirmation doesn't always look like an award.
> Sometimes it looks like a word.

DECEMBER 4

READ OUT LOUD: **Mark 4:22 (NLT)**

For everything that is hidden will eventually be brought into the open, and every secret will be brought to light.

Think of a matchstick. The first spark can be small. Give it the right fuel, and eventually the flame will burn by itself.

Think of a human mind. The first spark of discovery can be small. Give it the right fuel, and eventually the fire of inquiry will burn by itself.

The right fuel for a real fire is wood *and* oxygen. Just the wood is not enough. Oxygen is necessary for a flame, even though it looks and feels like ... nothing.

The right fuel for inquiry is information and time. Just the information is not enough. You also need time to process. Have patience. Time is necessary for learning, even though it looks and feels like ... nothing.

Don't underestimate the power of processing.
It lights the fire of inquiry.

PRAY THAT GOD WILL SHOW YOU WHERE THERE IS SPACE AND TIME FOR PROCESSING.

DECEMBER 5

READ OUT LOUD: **Philippians 3:12 (NLT)**

I don't mean to say that I have already achieved these things or that I have already reached perfection. But I press on to possess that perfection for which Christ Jesus first possessed me.

You don't have to be perfect when you can be excellent. View yourself with patience.

Striving toward excellence sets your face in the right direction.

A driver veers toward the wreck she sees on the highway. In the same way, focusing on your mistakes draws you to make them again and again.

Look straight ahead so that you can move forward to make fewer errors. You will never be free of them, but you can make them less and less.

At every opportunity, choose to dress, to behave, to speak with excellence.

You represent an excellent God.
Focus on Him, and you will be drawn to Him.

DECEMBER 6

READ OUT LOUD: 1 Corinthians 15:58 (NIV)

Therefore, my dear brothers and sisters, stand firm. Let nothing move you. Always give yourselves fully to the work of the Lord, because you know that your labor in the Lord is not in vain.

You invest so much time in your work and service. People who don't do what you do will not understand.

The time investment for good work and service is incredible. You do it because one glimpse, one taste, of growth is exhilarating to you. God feels the same way when He invests time in you and sees spiritual growth. He loves to watch you bloom. He waits patiently for it.

Expect progress and wait patiently for it. Sometimes you will see it soon, sometimes you will see it many years later. Sometimes you will not see it at all. But every undocumented hour of effort is worth spending.

God accepts your offering of time.
By giving time to those who are made in His image, you are giving it to Him.

DECEMBER 7

READ OUT LOUD: **Philippians 4:19 (CJB)**

Moreover, my God will fill every need of yours according to His glorious wealth, in union with the Messiah.

It is tempting to look around you and list the things you need. Even joking, saying things such as, "I need a live-in maid!" or "I need a personal assistant!" is a way of taking your eyes off of God. He has given you everything you need.

Change the way you think. Act from patience and contentment. When you identify a need, adopt a perspective of provision, saying, "It might feel like I need a live-in maid, but I am so thankful that God has given me arms and legs to get this work done. He has given me everything I need."

The more you thank Him for what He has already given you, the more your loving Father will be moved to give you more.

THANK GOD FOR FIVE BLESSINGS HE HAS GIVEN YOU.

1. _____
2. _____
3. _____
4. _____
5. _____

DECEMBER 8

READ OUT LOUD: **Proverbs 23:17-18 (NLT)**

Don't envy sinners, but always continue to fear the LORD. You will be rewarded for this; your hope will not be disappointed.

It can be disheartening when your expectations are shattered. In fact, it makes your heart feel sick. Proverbs 13:12 says: "Hope deferred makes the heart sick ..."

If you look around at others, it will compound that ill feeling. You see people who have the very thing you want, the thing you have been praying for. How long will you have to wait for God's promises to be fulfilled? *How long?* It hurts so badly because you thought something would have happened by now. Your expectations have not been met, and now you fear you will miss out altogether.

It seems like everyone is watching you hope. Public expectation feels embarrassing. What if you spend all this time waiting for something that never comes?

"Oh, forget it!" you want to say in frustration.

But God will not forget it.
Just wait.

DECEMBER 9

READ OUT LOUD: Romans 8:25 (NLT)

But if we look forward to something we don't yet have, we must wait patiently and confidently.

Have patience.

When God asks you to wait, upsetting the timetable of your expectations, it is because He is preparing you, preparing another person, or preparing a situation. There is always a reason. And it is not because He just didn't get that far down on His list of things-to-do today.

He knows you.
He loves you.

Your life is more than something for Him "to do."
He will act when the time is right.

IF GOD HAD A TO-DO LIST FOR YOUR HEART RIGHT NOW, WHAT WOULD BE ON IT?

1. _____
2. _____
3. _____
4. _____
5. _____

DECEMBER 10

READ OUT LOUD: Romans 8:22-23 (NLT)

For we know that all creation has been groaning as in the pains of childbirth right up to the present time. And we believers also groan, even though we have the Holy Spirit within us as a foretaste of future glory, for we long for our bodies to be released from sin and suffering. We, too, wait with eager hope for the day when God will give us our full rights as his adopted children including the new bodies he has promised us.

You do not have to be afraid of some discomfort. It doesn't always mean you are outside of God's will.

Sometimes it means you are *in* it.

See how a mother experiences discomfort during a birth? Periods of discomfort can bring new life to you, too.

Don't just wait, wait well.

IS THERE A CIRCUMSTANCE THAT IS CAUSING YOU DISCOMFORT? ASK GOD FOR SUPERNATURAL ENCOURAGEMENT SO THAT YOU CAN PERSEVERE.

DECEMBER 11

READ OUT LOUD: Galatians 6:9 (NIV)

Let us not become weary in doing good, for at the proper time we will reap a harvest if we do not give up.

One of the best ways that you can honor others is to wait patiently for them.

Wait for them to catch up. Wait for them to show progress. Wait for them to exhibit the improvement that you know will come.

To become impatient is to begin the process of giving up. You know that everyone grows at a different rate. Waiting patiently acknowledges and respects their individuality.

And what if the change would have come the very day *after* you gave up?

That is not a risk you can take.
Never give up.

WRITE ABOUT A TIME YOU WERE GLAD YOU DID NOT GIVE UP.

_____

_____

_____

_____

DECEMBER 12

READ OUT LOUD: Psalm 27:13-14 (NLT)

Yet I am confident I will see the Lord's goodness while I am here in the land of the living. Wait patiently for the Lord. Be brave and courageous. Yes, wait patiently for the Lord.

One might assume that the opposite of pride is humility. Perhaps the opposite of pride is patience. Patience proceeds at a steady pace, partnering with God. Pride hurries ahead of God.

It takes patience to finish, but God will see it—and see *you*—through.

LIST THREE AREAS IN WHICH YOU ARE COMMITTED TO WAITING ON GOD.

1. _____
2. _____
3. _____

DECEMBER 13

READ OUT LOUD: Philippians 4:6 (NLT)

Don't worry about anything; instead, pray about everything. Tell God what you need, and thank him for all He has done.

You know that you can work more quickly with people who cooperate.

Sometimes God would be able to work more quickly with you if you would cooperate.

He loves you and is thinking of you constantly, planning surprises and delights. His training may feel uncomfortable at times, but it will never harm you.

You don't have to question His motives. He always has your best at heart. Draw near to Him the way you would a trusted tutor, ready to learn.

And thank Him for what He has already taught you.

WHAT ARE THREE IMPORTANT LESSONS YOU HAVE LEARNED?

1. _____
2. _____
3. _____

DECEMBER 14

READ OUT LOUD: Ecclesiastes 7:9 (MSG)

Don't be quick to fly off the handle. Anger boomerangs. You can spot a fool by the lumps on his head.

Exercise patience in the day-to-day, moment-to-moment duties of your life.

There will be times you will want to explode in frustration, but anything that comes out of your mouth always comes back to you. Make sure what you give is something you wouldn't mind receiving.

If you have recently been a little testy with others, there are six magic phrases that will work miracles in restoring relationship:

Please.
Thank you.
I'm sorry.
How can I help?
I care about you.
Let's work together.

Pick two or three of these and begin a conversation.

WHAT ARE SOME OTHER SMALL PHRASES THAT MAKE A BIG DIFFERENCE?

1. _____
2. _____
3. _____

DECEMBER 15

READ OUT LOUD: Ephesians 4:2b (NLT)

Be patient with each other, making allowance for each other's faults because of your love.

Chances are, you have experienced a time when mercy and grace were the only things you wanted.

The human tendency is to think that if you offer mercy and grace, an offensive behavior will keep happening. However, you know from experience that sometimes receiving mercy and grace was enough to make you *never* want to repeat a behavior again.

There are times when correction is called for, but there are *more times* when mercy and grace are the order of the day.

Extend to others what you would want extended to you: patience.

USING INITIALS ONLY, PRAY FOR A COLLEAGUE WHO COULD USE A LITTLE PATIENCE FROM OTHERS.

DECEMBER 16

READ OUT LOUD: 1 Peter 2:19-20 (NLT)

For God is pleased when, conscious of his will, you patiently endure unjust treatment. Of course, you get no credit for being patient if you are beaten for doing wrong. But if you suffer for doing good and endure it patiently, God is pleased with you.

It is guaranteed that there will be times when you are treated unfairly.

When that happens, the knee-jerk response is to become indignant and guard your position.

If you have done nothing wrong and are suffering for it, then turn to God, your heavenly Advocate. He is pleased when His followers exercise patience.

Trust Him to defend you instead of trying to defend yourself.

BY THE POWER OF JESUS, PRAY FOR AND BLESS THE PERSON WHO HAS TREATED YOU UNFAIRLY. YOU WILL RECEIVE WHAT YOU ASK FOR ON THEIR BEHALF, AS WELL.

_____

_____

_____

_____

_____

_____

DECEMBER 17

READ OUT LOUD: Romans 5:4 (NLT)

And endurance develops strength of character, and character strengthens our confident hope of salvation.

Exercising patience is part of your character training. You do not have to be afraid of the *need* for patience. You do not have to avoid situations that *require* patience.

The Lord may ask you to practice certain character concepts. Patience can be learned, over time. You will become better at it.

Before you start thinking your character is just fine the way it is, realize that the purpose of refining your character is to bring about more hope in your life. Hope does not disappoint.

The next time you face a big challenge, whisper under your breath:
This is just an exercise.
This is just an exercise.
This is just an exercise.

Practice will improve your patience.

DECEMBER 18

READ OUT LOUD: Proverbs 3:5-8a (MSG)

Trust God from the bottom of your heart; don't try to figure out everything on your own. Listen for God's voice in everything you do, everywhere you go; He's the one who will keep you on track. Don't assume that you know it all. Run to God! Run from evil! Your body will glow with health, your very bones will vibrate with life!

Trust brings refreshment.

Trust brings renewal and vivacity.

That is what God promises. Doubting takes a lot of work and worry, and if you trade your doubt for simple trust, there are benefits to your physical health that will be visible almost immediately.

Be patient. Trust Him today.

Feel the difference when you put down the weight of your life.

PUT DOWN THE HEAVINESS OF THREE THINGS ON YOUR MIND TODAY. ENTRUST THEM TO GOD IN PRAYER.

1. _____
2. _____
3. _____

DECEMBER 19

READ OUT LOUD: James 1:19 (NLT)

Understand this, my dear brothers and sisters: You must all be quick to listen, slow to speak, and slow to get angry.

Few people are proficient listeners. Most would admit they are better talkers.

This week, exhibit patience by choice. Look for opportunities to listen. Listen actively in meetings. Try to focus for an entire day on listening more than you talk.

Let listening to others teach you about yourself.

THANK GOD FOR THREE PEOPLE WHO HAVE BEEN GOOD LISTENERS IN YOUR LIFE.

1. _____
2. _____
3. _____

DECEMBER 20

READ OUT LOUD: Luke 12:11b-12 (NIV)

... do not worry about ... what you will say for the Holy Spirit will teach you at that time what you need to say.

Regret happens *after* an event. It is rehashing and rehashing and rehashing what you wish you had done or said.

Regret is *rewinding.*

Rumination happens *before* an event. It is rehearsing and rehearsing and rehearsing what you plan to do or say.

Ruminating is *fast-forwarding.*

Neither rehashing nor rehearsing will help. Both regret and rumination keep your focus somewhere other than where you are *right now.* Don't rewind your life, and certainly don't fast-forward it.

Your words do not have to be perfect. You do not have to practice the conversation prior to actually having it. Be patient with yourself.

Let God put the words into your mouth when you need them.

He rarely supplies them a moment sooner.

DECEMBER 21

READ OUT LOUD: Proverbs 15:18 (NIV)

A hot-tempered person stirs up conflict, but the one who is patient calms a quarrel.

What a valuable friend you will be if you are the one who quiets a quarrel first. Arguments happen so quickly and get out of hand before you know it. Often, the disagreement itself becomes bigger than the original reason behind it.

If you show patience ... if you wait a day before responding, you may find that the conflict dies down on its own.

An argument needs fuel.
The patient person refuses to supply it.

WHAT IS A PRACTICAL THING YOU CAN DO THE NEXT TIME YOU ARE TEMPTED TO ENGAGE IN A DISAGREEMENT?

DECEMBER 22

READ OUT LOUD: Isaiah 40:31 (NLT)

But those who trust in the Lord will find new strength. They will soar high on wings like eagles. They will run and not grow weary. They will walk and not faint.

God does not expect you to generate your own patience. He richly gives you all you need.

The key to unlocking His storehouse is to actually *need* what is behind those doors and ask for it. He has no reason to pour out an abundance of patience upon someone who is not being tested. Neither does He hurry to pour out patience upon someone who does not ask for it in prayer.

God is the most patient of all.

He wants a trusting relationship with you, and He is willing to wait for it to grow.

ASK GOD FOR PATIENCE.

DECEMBER 23

READ OUT LOUD: Psalm 37:7 (NLT)

Be still in the presence of the Lord, and wait patiently for him to act. Don't worry about evil people who prosper or fret about their wicked schemes.

It is easy to think that your success comes from your own efforts. No, true success can only come from cooperation with God. The tricky thing about partnering with God is that you are on the grace of His timetable.

This is always a blessing, but doesn't always feel like one.

When you don't see something happening, you might think that *nothing* is happening. Waiting on God is like being on a train; you sit still, while being carried along at 70 miles per hour by a powerful engine.

You are moving forward as you wait, but it feels like you aren't doing anything but sitting still right now. The truth is, the season of waiting on the Lord is the most important time of all. This is when you can do effective spiritual work.

You can pray. This is not begging. It is blessing. Bless the situation. Bless yourself. Bless everyone involved.

Prayer will always test your mettle.

It will make you into the person you need to be by the time the answer comes.

DECEMBER **24**

READ OUT LOUD: James 1:4 (NKJV)

But let patience have its perfect work, that you may be perfect and complete, lacking nothing.

As if God has not given you enough of a gift in His Son, He gives you one more: the gift of yourself.

He knows how He created you. He always meant for you to be a reflection of His image. He loves you and watches over you with care.

He wants you to be able to see who you were meant to be. One way that He does that is by opening your heart. When you are going through something difficult, He allows you to see what is really in your heart. Your heart is beautiful to Him. Is it beautiful to you? Ask for eyes to see yourself the way He sees you.

The parts that need perfecting, will be perfected. Patience will do what He means for it to do in you.

Not one moment of your life will be wasted.
Even the days you have spent waiting.

DECEMBER 25

READ OUT LOUD: Romans 8:22 (NIV)

We know that the whole creation has been groaning as the pains of childbirth right up to the present time.

A mother waits expectantly for the birth of her child. The closer the pregnancy nears its final hours, the harder it is to wait.

Like Jesus' mother received her divine assignment with patience and surrender, may you accept the challenging task that God is asking of you today.

May you carry it to completion with the endurance of Mary.

The birth of God's plan will be worth the patience required to deliver it.

THANK GOD FOR TWO SIGNIFICANT THINGS THAT HE HAS BIRTHED IN YOUR LIFE THIS YEAR.

1. _____
2. _____

DECEMBER 26

READ OUT LOUD: James 5:7 (NIV)

Be patient, then, brothers and sisters, until the Lord's coming. See how the farmer waits for the land to yield its valuable crop, patiently waiting for the autumn and spring rains.

The Fruit of the Spirit is worth cultivating. Love, joy, peace, patience, kindness, goodness, faithfulness, gentleness, and self-control ... all of these are attributes that you want and need.

If you see an area in your life where one of these spiritual character traits is weak, then ask for more fruit. Some people say they are afraid of asking for patience because then the Lord will give them more situations that require patience. That may be true, but you never have to fear anything that the Lord would give you.

He is the Master Gardener, and He knows how to handle delicate blooms without harming them. He knows how to make them—to make *you*—more abundant.

He knows how to help you grow in the most *loving, joyful, peaceful, patient, kind, good, faithful, gentle, self-controlled* way.

Jesus is patient. He won't push you.
Remember, He bears the Fruit of the Spirit, too.

DECEMBER 27

READ OUT LOUD: Proverbs 16:33 (NIV)

The lot is cast into the lap, but its every decision is from the Lord.

One of the biggest tragedies of our lives is one decision away. Every day, we have to make that very decision—*will we give up?*

Giving up is the ultimate way to be held back from God's best for our lives. Giving up ensures that God will never have a chance to heal, to restore, to renew, to surprise, to reward, to make things any different for us than they are today.

People give up because they think "it" will never happen. People give up because they have banked on a dream or desire that they *think* is their own. They think it is their own dream to start dreaming and their own dream to stop dreaming.

But what if it isn't yours? What if God is the One who placed that glowing hope in your heart? What if your dream is not yours, at all, but is His dream for you? What if He has entrusted it to you, and is waiting for you to entrust it back to Him?

Will you give up on it now?

Treasure God's dream for you.
Keep it until He completes it.

DECEMBER 28

READ OUT LOUD: 2 Peter 3:9 (NIV)

The Lord is not slow in keeping his promise, as some understand slowness. Instead he is patient with you, not wanting anyone to perish, but everyone to come to repentance.

Your definition of timeliness and God's are much different.

As you face the new year and begin thinking about New Year's resolutions, you might feel some sadness about what you did *not* accomplish since your last set of New Year's resolutions.

Realize that it is not over yet. You are just refreshing and rebooting, that's all. Even if you did not complete what you set out to do at the beginning of this year, surrender those first small efforts to God. He saw your intentions. He saw how you got off to a good start. He heard your prayers and will continue to fulfill those prayers over time.

Make some of the same New Year's resolutions this year if you want to. Just because you didn't achieve them in one year's time does not mean that you will not achieve them at all.

God is patient.
In time, He will help you conquer everything you commit to Him.

DECEMBER 29

READ OUT LOUD: Matthew 20:26-28 (NIV)

Not so with you. Instead, whoever wants to become great among you must be your servant, and whoever wants to be first must be your slave—just as the Son of Man did not come to be served, but to serve, and to give his life as a ransom for many.

The way to rise as a person of influence is to make yourself low, to serve without ulterior motives, to seek to improve the lives of others. This way is opposite of what the world teaches. The world suggests that you pull away from the pack in order to be noticed. Jesus points to a different paradigm. The Kingdom of God is one of paradox.

Patiently serving will increase your influence over time.

People are quick to listen to someone who has their best interests at heart.

WRITE DOWN FOUR WAYS THAT YOU CAN SERVE AND BLESS THE PEOPLE AROUND YOU TODAY. THEN DO IT.

1. _____
2. _____
3. _____
4. _____

DECEMBER 30

READ OUT LOUD: Revelation 2:19 (NIV)

I know your deeds, your love and faith, your service and perseverance, and that you are now doing more than you did at first.

God sees your every effort. No act of love is beyond His notice. He sees what you do and is pleased, the same way that you are pleased when your own children have shown improvement. You know they don't have to be all the way there in order to bring a smile to your face. You enjoy watching them inch along the path of progress. You remember where they have been, even as you can see where they are going.

As you prepare for a new season, think about how far *you* have come. You have inched along the path of progress, too.

SET A TIMER FOR FIFTEEN MINUTES, SIT DOWN, WRITE IN A JOURNAL WITHOUT SELF-EDITING. JUST POUR OUT YOUR HEART. WHAT ARE YOU DOING NOW THAT YOU WERE NOT DOING AT THE BEGINNING OF THIS YEAR? HOW HAVE YOU IMPROVED? BE STILL AND ASK THE LORD TO DIRECT YOUR THOUGHTS ON THIS. HE MAY WANT TO CALL TO YOUR MIND A FEW AREAS OF PERSONAL SUCCESS THAT YOU HAVE OVERLOOKED.

DECEMBER 31

READ OUT LOUD: Hebrews 12:1 (NLT)

Therefore, since we are surrounded by such a huge crowd of witnesses to the life of faith, let us strip off every weight that slows us down, especially the sin that so easily trips us up. And let us run with endurance the race God has set before us.

Enter the new year with new hope. Look behind only for a moment, to see how far you have come.

Avoid looking back to regret.

Avoid looking back to complain.

Avoid looking back to wonder if things could have been different.

This is a long race. It is a marathon, not a sprint. You will need to keep your eyes ahead in order to run it well.

If you feel concerned about things that did not go as you hoped, don't waste another moment on worry. There is still time. Get ready to approach the spring with fervor. Plan now how you will nourish yourself: body, mind, heart, and spirit. Add meaningful self-care as part of your New Year's resolutions. Let God pour renewed energy into you today.

Don't fold your arms in frustration about last year.

A new year is coming, and with it, a new way.

ABOUT THE AUTHOR

When I was 20 years old, my plans for my life, career, family, and future fell apart. I was an active sophomore in college, then suddenly I was quadriplegic in the Intensive Care Unit, having suffered a massive brainstem stroke. I could not speak, swallow, or blink. My faith sustained me in ways I can hardly explain, and a year later I walked back onto my college campus on my own two feet. Now I hold a BS in mass communications from Texas Wesleyan University and an MA in English education from Columbia University.

I taught in public schools for ten years, and in private schools for two more. In 2007, the Texas Education Agency awarded me the distinguished honor of Texas Secondary Teacher of the Year. Currently, I write and speak full time, sharing messages of hope and endurance with education, business, and church groups. Almost everyone walks away with a renewed sense of purpose.

All of my communication—books, keynote speeches, products, podcasts, and workshops—centers on practicing hope and endurance. I have learned that even when a situation seems impossible, it is never too late. But in order to persevere, people need a steady supply of encouragement. Whenever I can, I want to be someone who offers it.

―― ALSO BY NIKA MAPLES ――

KEEP TEACHING
NIKA MAPLES

As an educator, you bring your whole heart to school every day. But how can you keep your heart as healthy as possible? Reading Scripture over yourself and your classroom is one simple way to bring miraculous growth and sustainability. You want to be effective, and there is nothing like the equipping power of God's Word to stregnthen you.

Use *Keep Teaching* as a daily devotional book that centers your thoughts on Jesus any time during the school day. With 365 Bible verses and insightful devotional thoughts, you will find enough grace to take you from the first day of school to the longest days of summer. *Keep Teaching* is filled with prayer prompts, moments of meditation, and brief spaces for reflection, making it a book you will want to keep as close as your coffee cup.

EVERYDAY GENESIS
NIKA MAPLES

Do you desire to change or completely start over? Starting over is not as difficult as we think. The Genesis account of Creation reveals a divine sequence, showing us the secrets to new life. When we invite the Creator to make us new, we release any blame and regret we carry and embrace His foundation for re-creation, a new life. There we find exactly Who was presiding over the genesis of the earth.

He can re-create us with a similar process: first bringing us revelation, then giving us benefits such as purpose and guidance, and finally teaching us to build a legacy. Through the divine sequence of Creation, we can learn simple spiritual disciplines for abiding in Christ and staying in step with the Spirit. If we want to begin again, we start at the Beginning.

HUNTING HOPE
NIKA MAPLES

When you are experiencing a season of difficulty and hope is hard to find, hunt for it by holding onto God's character and letting Him reveal all the possibilities you can't even imagine.

At twenty years of age, when all hope seemed lost, Nika Maples searched for it boldly and defied all odds to recover from a devastating stroke that left her unable to walk, speak, or even blink. The lessons from that struggle are powerful and universal.

In *Hunting Hope*, Nika uses real life examples and biblical insight to show you how to become a hope hunter by seeking God when you feel surrounded by darkness. As you read Nika's journey, you'll learn to rest in the assurance that--even while living in hardship--there is always hope in Christ.

TWELVE CLEAN PAGES
NIKA MAPLES

Imprisoned in her own body by a paralyzing stroke at age twenty, Nika Maples depended upon spiritual strength in order to surmount the greatest challenge of her young life: standing on her own two feet again. Not only did she stand, obliterating doctors' initial prognoses, she walked ... directly into the passionate profession of a public high school teacher.

Thirteen years after the medical trauma she was not expected to survive, Nika stood inside the glimmering granite capitol building in Austin, honored to receive state House and Senate resolutions as 2007 Texas Secondary Teacher of the Year. Let your heart rise along with the inspirational account of a single mother's faith, her dying daughter's hope, and God's triumphant love.

www.ingramcontent.com/pod-product-compliance
Lightning Source LLC
Chambersburg PA
CBHW020900080526
44589CB00011B/368